T0283854

TWENTY SQUARE FEET OF SKIN

21ST CENTURY ESSAYS
David Lazar and Patrick Madden, Series Editors

TWENTY SQUARE FEET OF SKIN

MEGAN BAXTER

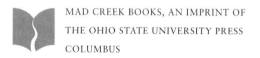

MAD CREEK BOOKS, AN IMPRINT OF
THE OHIO STATE UNIVERSITY PRESS
COLUMBUS

Library of Congress Cataloging-in-Publication Data
available online at https://catalog.loc.gov
LCCN: 2022051217

Identifiers: ISBN 978-0-8142-5868-2 (paper);
ISBN 978-0-8142-8283-0 (ebook)

Cover design by Derek Thornton
Text design by Juliet Williams
Type set in Sabon

♾ The paper used in this publication meets the minimum requirements of the
American National Standard for Information Sciences—Permanence of Paper
for Printed Library Materials. ANSI Z39.48-1992.

CONTENTS

A DELIBERATE THING I SAID ONCE TO MY SKIN

To consider my tattoos we must first consider skin. Skin is our barrier against the world, enveloping our body so that we won't lose our precious water and evaporate like dew. The outer layer, the epidermis, lacks blood vessels and survives on oxygen alone, although it needs very little of it because many of its cells are already dead. A skin cell lives for a fortnight and is then pressed upward through the process of desquamation to flake off and float around your house as dust.

The strata of our skin resemble slices of the earth, where twenty-five to thirty layers of skin cells separate us from the outside world. Scratch your epidermis and you might flake off a few dead cells, but cut into your dermis and you'll bleed and slap your hand to the cut in pain. It is in the dermis that tattoo ink is deposited and where, as the years of a life progress, the ink sinks like heavy water, fading away through layers of skin like a figure retreating into shadow.

There are marks that fate applied to our bodies: freckles, moles, and scars—from falls, mean housecats, sharp kitchen knives, and slippery rocks in the water holes where we learned to swim—and then there are marks we etch into our skin deliberately: razor nicks, piercings, tattoos.

The average adult lives within twenty square feet of skin, roughly the size of a large baby blanket, although shaped, of course, not like a blanket but like a human. A big canvas. Skin covered in ink doesn't much resemble our naked dead layers. It looks like snake and bird feather, scale and leather.

Tattoos are often the language of the dead because skin can speak for us when we are gone. Sailors hoped their ink would identify their bodies if they drowned at sea. Salt and water do horrible things to a body, erasing all personality, removing eyes, wiping faces clean, but even stretched and water-logged a tattoo remains locked in flesh.

Anchors, pirate queens, bleeding hearts—all offered something like an ID card. For the inked mummies of the Euro-Asian steppe and the bodies of the Iceman and an Egyptian priestess . . . what did their dots and dashes and their swirling chimerical animals mean to their owners? Perhaps only that they had names, even in death.

I am certain that I began drawing on myself early. I drew on all things, so it seems fitting that my skin was also my canvas. In school I doodled on my hands and arms, writing notes that blossomed into flowers and vines. But that ink scrubbed away or smeared off on my cheek in the night. Like most kids who grew up in the country, I was checked with scars on my arms and legs from bike accidents, barbed wire, the blade of the pocketknife I had stolen from my father, a fishhook, a mean pine bough, the barbs of blackberry and raspberry bushes.

My skin, if I consider it, is not particularly special. It is neither oily nor dry. It isn't a large hide, not quite twenty square feet, and beyond the scratches and scrapes of child-hood it has escaped real damage, enduring only moderate acne during adolescence and again during a rough spot in my late twenties.

But I am inscribed with images, electric with ink. See me naked, or moving through the water, swimming in clear lakes, see me in a sundress or walking the trash to the curb, see me stretching my muscles toward the sun, see me showering off the sweat of the day, and see my arms and legs illustrated, my back and foot patterned, my hipbone stamped with pigment, my shoulder opening wings of ink.

> *I am the poet of the body, And I am the poet of the soul,*
> *The pleasures of heaven are with me, and the pains of*
> *   hell are with me,*
> *The first I graft and increase upon myself—the latter I*
> *   translate into a new tongue.*
>   —Walt Whitman

Whitman might have seen tattoos in the hospital wards on the limbs of those dying boys that he tended with letters and words and ice cream. Martin Hildebrandt, a tattoo artist from New York City, enlisted in the Army of the Potomac and was known to ink men so that their bodies might be identified. There were no dog tags in the Civil War, and despite a six-year program undertaken in 1865 by the Quartermaster General to locate and inter the dead, only half of the war's fatalities were identified.

The first tattoo, a cross on my hipbone. My mother accompanied me because I was under eighteen, and she was trying, with her first and most willful child, to be cool. She talked the artist down to inking me with something no bigger than a quarter. It was over before I understood the pain. The waistline of my jeans wore it off over the course of a two-week hiking trip that I embarked on just after getting the tattoo. It was cloudy and mosaicked before I had it reworked four months later when I sat for my second tattoo. The man let me tattoo myself while he took a break to relax his hands. He guided me through the process as his feet pumped the machine.

"You came into the world perfect," my mother muttered, after each tattoo, in protest.

Consider pain. Consider the skin under pain. That organ is the perfect vehicle for agony. It can be burned, cut, rubbed off, frozen, lashed, electrified, beaten, pierced, branded. There is pain in the skin; there has to be for us to walk through the world and know fire and ice and to pick up things like marbles and bowling balls and to tie shoelaces or zip up a dress. It is our barrier, but it screams to us; those nerves woven through the dermis shoot electric warnings to our distant brains. Many tortures have been enacted upon skin. The saints at their martyrdom. The Death by a Thousand Cuts. The mind has dreamed up and then executed a thousand violations of that greatest of organs, that membrane that protects the individual from the universe.

Perhaps tired of traditional methods, or simply crueler than the rest, the Byzantine Emperor Theophilos had the brothers Theophanes and Theodore tortured for their protest against iconoclasm. Over the course of two days he had their faces tattooed with twelve lines of his metrically correct, although artistically unsuccessful, poetry. The brothers survived and continued their protests. Later, when they were venerated as saints, they became known as the Grapti, the "written upon" or "the inscribed."

There is a comma missing in the poem on my left leg. I didn't notice it was missing until a few months later. I have a very casual relationship with commas and am surprised I took note. Sometimes I draw it in with pen, but to have it fixed permanently seems so fussy.

> Stay together [missing comma] learn the flowers, go
>   light.
>
> —Gary Snyder

There is a line through the dark image on my left shoulder that a beloved cat tore as he escaped from my arms and into the yard at dusk. That too will remain while the image on my back simply fades away. That tattoo, a Celtic knot, sits on the sliver of skin that is exposed by my shirt hiking up my back as I lean forward to weed or plant. It has faded so that when I am deep summer tanned it appears more like an elaborate birth mark than a tattoo; it is a memory of a deliberate thing I said once to my skin forever.

The pain of fading, the pain of mistake, is not as bad as the pain at its origin under the needle. Have you ever picked a scab and pulled its crust too deep? Have you felt the bite of a razor on your anklebone and a rush of sweet sharp something too? Can there be love without this exposure, or growth without that tingling ache in the bones? There are scales for pain, but they aren't accurate. Each body has its own measure, and year to year, place to place on our hide, it changes. Consider the inside of your elbow or the smooth skin along your ribs, both dangerously sensitive to the needle so that some artists won't touch you there for your first tattoo. Now run your hands over your deltoid and biceps, the rounded head of your shoulder and the meaty part of your upper arm, the skin on your calf. Thick and distant from bone. Here the needle sinks without getting too close to the tender parts. Here you'll not feel it shake your skeleton.

Sometimes a cat scratch. Sometimes a burn. The needle will bite and then radiate out as the minutes become hours, until the whole thing is a flooded field of red, raw pain. A tattoo's pain can ache downward from the dermis to the muscle fiber to the bone. It'll start to move. Or maybe that's the pain from not moving, from sitting and becoming canvas. But even if you stretch, even if the artist offers you a Coca Cola for the sugar rush, even if he leaves you for a while to smoke a cigarette or answer the phone, the skin will buzz. The needle vibrates like bees in the grass. Its hiss shocks you at first and you'll jump, but that's just the beginning. Then you'll know how it hurts. Then you'll know how a good artist will start light and then press deeper or start with the single needled outliner and finish with the many needled shader, scratching in ink instead of drawing it like a fine-tipped pen across your bloody skin.

But the pain is essential. It releases endorphins that flood you with something like love and joy. A two-beer buzz. Sex. French fries and milkshakes. The good stuff. And after a while you won't be able to describe the pain, but you'll know that it is a key, and the release is worth the scratch.

Unscrew the locks from the doors!
Unscrew the doors themselves from their jambs!
—*Walt Whitman*

I am an addict. I think I should say that. I fall hard for things, and I've had to cut them out too. Booze and cigarettes are gone now. I have to watch that I don't get too involved with pastimes. Too interested. I'll pick at a scab until it becomes a scar. I'll keep looking for that sweet response. I know that.

Some people get addicted to tattoos. I have seven, the large one on my left arm being, what I consider now, my last. The pain was never that much of a high for me. Except during that last one, when—like a terrible night of drinking when you cheat on your beloved and crash your car and then swear never to touch the bottle again—I found the edge of my tolerance for the needle. That tattoo ink was cut with witch hazel to help me heal, but Oh! the sting! And the single session lasted nine hours, instead of being broken into the normal two four-hour sessions, because the artist was leaving the next day. He began in the meaty part of my arm and finished in the tender bits—my armpit, my elbow bone, until I rang with pain—inking in an image from an illustrated edition of *Leaves of Grass,* women holding babies, men pushing plows, birds breaking into the sky of my shoulder. Driving home delirious, I wondered if I might not be breaking the law.

Consider inspiration. Is it born in a dream or myth or pretty picture you saw once? I rolled my tattoos around in my mind for years before they spread out on my skin, except for one. The eagle on my shoulder landed on me.

There are seasons marked on my body like a castaway's notches to record the day. The Celtic cross and knots. The poets: Jeffers (his red-tailed hawk), Snyder, and Whitman.

In the season of the eagle tattoo, my heart was freshly broken, and I was driving out west hoping hard to find adventure, or at least something other than the snow of another New England winter. Over the mountain passes of the Rockies I prayed for my car's engine. I wrote in cheap motel rooms and hoped someone would text or call me, but my phone was silent. To anyone who asked, I told lies about who I was and what I was doing, as if I were trying on different skins, but the one thing that stayed with me, state to state, dawn to dusk, were the eagles. I saw them, or they saw me and followed me west, their white hooded heads sharp against the sky.

I joked that I would get an image of one of them inked on my arm. Joked to the tracks of Lynyrd Skynyrd and the Allman Brothers. Joked to the stale air in my car.

In Utah I settled into a nest of a motel room a few minutes away from the gates of Zion. I could see the rim of some red rock formation from the window near my desk. The sun cast over its face like clock hands counting away hours. And the eagles hung above it, screaming silent in the desert sky. No, not screaming. Yipping. Hawks scream. Eagles yip like beagles.

When I couldn't write a word, I drove. My car red with dust, I followed a brochure's map up a dirt road on the other side of Zion National Park. It was the last day of the year. A man in a silver pickup truck looked down, worried, into my window as we passed on the tight road. As he drove down to the main highway I saw that his bed was full of hound dogs, their noses pressed to the grates of their cage.

The road ended or seemed to end at the gates of Grafton, a historic site, a ghost town whose fields were still farmed by a rancher down the valley. Walking the main road, I felt like I'd been there before. Miles Romney, an architect sent by Brigham Young to oversee the construction of the St. George Temple, was housed in Grafton while final plans were drawn up. He wrote in his journal, "When I studied Milton's *Paradise Lost* in school I never intended to spend the last part of my life in it." The settlement spread out on the skirts of the Virgin River, with the red cliffs behind and the clear sky above. Red, green, blue cut boldly into the earth. But it wasn't beauty that made me pause, for the West has plenty of that. I knew those old buildings worn by the desert sun. I knew the church and schoolhouse, the fences and barns.

An eagle circled. Hunting.

Then it came to me, but I didn't believe myself until I read it in the fine print at the bottom of the historical society's sign. Grafton had been featured in several movies, most notably *Butch Cassidy and the Sundance Kid*. The gentle schoolteacher Etta lived in this paradise, and the outlaws came to her for food and love and shelter. Dusty, Redford, and Newman dragged themselves to the light of that house while the posse, nameless, faceless, bore down on them.

"There are no second acts in American lives," F. Scott Fitzgerald said, but Butch and Sundance got one by running away and living in Bolivia for over a decade before they were killed. Or not. Lula Parker, Butch's sister, claimed that he returned to Utah and died there of old age. In the movie they live forever in that long, frozen shot as they blast out into the marketplace where the Bolivian Army's rifles can be heard. There's no pain in that ending.

I've always loved that movie. Its evasion and veiled truth. Once I dreamt of Whitman and Galway Kinnell holed up together, bandaging their wounds, talking not of Australia and banks but of the body and the soul. I've read that hearing other people's dreams is boring, but I can't imagine why. I consider this dreamed scene often: on the count of three the poets run out into the bullets and are frozen there on the screen.

> *I believe in the flesh and the appetites,*
> *Seeing, hearing, feeling, are miracles, and each part and*
> *   tag of me is a miracle.*
> *Divine am I inside and out, and I make holy whatever I*
> *   touch or am touched from,*
> *The scent of these armpits aroma finer than prayer,*
> *This head more than churches, bibles, and all the creeds.*
> —Walt Whitman

My body the only universe I'll really inhabit. And what have I inked upon it?

> *I have come to myself empty, the rope strung out behind*
> *   me*
> *in the fall sun*
> *suddenly glorified with all my blood.*
> —Galway Kinnell

I wanted blood in Utah, and tattooing is a bloody art. As the needle tears into the dermis, blood wells up and things get messy. The artist smears your skin with vitamin A and D ointment, which helps keep the blood down but not enough; they'll wipe it away every few minutes with a paper towel so that briefly they can see the image they're carving.

Imagine having something to write but nothing to write on or with. You go tearing into your desk for a pen and paper.

You rattle through all the stuff in your purse, the glove box, and you feel the words pounding on your skull demanding to be inscribed. *Eagle. Eagle. Eagle,* my skin said. *Eagle my skin,* I said.

Somewhere between magic and mysticism, truth is suspended. Magic is just a trick you haven't figured out yet. Mystics are something else entirely. They can talk to God and animals. Their dreams are worth paying attention to. When they die their skin becomes leather. Their bones are good luck. Their poems cause people to sway and see the Virgin Mary or taste spring water on their lips. There isn't any reason in them, though if there is, it is mythic reason, full moon thought, and tidal. Theirs is the way of the spirit. They might begin as blank canvases, but they become saints.

I don't believe in magic. I think it's a silly thing to even have to say. When I was three, to save me from having to believe a lie, my father told me Santa was fake. But I believe in the body and the spirit and the skin living on air as it separates us from air, and in things that I don't understand pulling at me. I can't really tell you how the tides work, but I know they are called by the moon's gravity and that the lunar cycle tugs at the blood in my belly too. I don't speak Eagle, but the eagles told me to get back in my car and drive down I-15, to St. George, where I would find a man with ink in his needle— on this, the last day of the year of our Lord, 2009.

Tattoo shops, or parlors, or studios, are not welcoming places to walk into. Like all places that deal in blood, they are often tucked up in the armpits or off to the side of cities—especially nice cities, like St. George, where you can see Miles Romney's beautiful white temple or walk over the tracks of Jurassic reptiles at the Dinosaur Museum. To find a tattoo shop, you have to look for one. I followed a bumper sticker to a phone book to a strip mall where the only tattoo parlor open on New Year's Eve let me slip in as the last skin of the day. The place was tile and fifties roadster revival, but empty, and the man who inked my shoulder was the owner of the store.

In the past, I had always walked in with artwork, something I had drawn that had been waiting for flesh, but in Utah I knew only the bird and where it would soar on my body. He drew me an eagle and placed it, in temporary ink, with its wings over my upper arm. It wrapped me up lovingly.

First the hair is shaved. Human skin, like that of most mammals, is hairy, even if those hairs are fine and light, and these tiny hairs will get caught in ink and needle. Then the rubbing of alcohol swabs, the cleansing. I settled forward in the chair, my arm outstretched. He assembled his kit. The ink quaked, dark in its reservoirs. He banded the needle's necks to the machine and tapped it to life with his foot. Ointment was slathered over the site. He pulled at my shoulder, testing its elasticity, its thickness, its bounce. Then ink into needle and needle into skin, the first touch a cut to form a wing, a test, then faster and longer with each line until the bird is outlined. My blood wells so ruby, so shocking, dripping in orbs then messy with black ink.

A tattoo is a wound. Consider that you have just opened yourself to infection on the very surface that is meant to protect you from the world. You are now vulnerable in a way you weren't thirty minutes ago. The artist cleans the eagle up good and smears it with ointment, then he packs it away under a dressing and tapes the edges shut. The pain has made me excited. I shake as I drive away, back north to my motel. There are lights in the desert. The night is dark already when I arrive and peel the bandage off and gaze into the floor-length mirror. The eagle is part blood, part ink.

> *If I worship one thing more than another it shall be the*
> *spread of my own body.*
>
> —*Walt Whitman*

First the ink will rise up, and the image will be branded on you. Then it'll scab, but don't scratch it. It'll peel, but don't pull it. One by one the lines will fall away, and you will feel again your skin, smooth but full of ink now. The ink settles heavy in the dermis. Sitting above nerve and fat but below the dead layers that wear off. Deep enough to be forever in you.

Perhaps skin is the best place to be selfish. Under the dermis of our hands, we form the distinctive hurricanes of our fingerprints. These marks are created in the womb during the first trimester, and they remain with us, unchanged, through all seasons. Unique. Pressed in ink, they are our identity. We are known through our skin.

ON PLUCKING WHITE HAIRS

In the mirror, my eyes wear from searching silver out from the darkness. When I catch myself in the pupil, I see through and past, blurry until focus locks. If I stare long enough, one thing becomes another. I am a girl, a child, a photograph's white eye. It's not a trick of the mind, just exhaustion like any other folding of one memory into another. I have to grab hold of something steady to know myself and then pull back and out again. I am a woman, breath fogging the mirror glass, golden tweezers slipping silver hairs from the thick wax of her skull.

The body operates on its own timeline, some seasons draw long, and others shorten like a drought year's tree ring. The more I focus, the more I find between the roots. There's nothing essential in the ritual, it's just a simple outward-facing reward. But recently something other than beauty and its sharp hook have snagged me as I search out the white. When my eyes shift into focus and hold themselves stiff in the mirror, I catch her, just past the ghost of myself as a girl.

It's been years since I've seen Abby with my own two eyes (as they say), but I've held her image in my palm—watched her grow, marry, mother—on the reflective screen of my phone. Her eyes cracked, slowing into fine lines, crow's feet gathering up her freckles, her dark hair spun through with silver after the baby. She sets down the camera phone and takes selfies with her young daughter. In these snapshots, her eyes, looking at themselves on the screen, boomerang, matching my eyes in the mirror. Out and in and tumbling toward some kind of togetherness.

Abby, I think, as I shiver to grab a tail of silver, eyes up, and then falling, focusing. I knew myself by her until I lost that map, and although we share a birth year our bodies keep different times. As a girl, I could have counted the freckles on her face like we numbered stars in the night sky. She grew tall the summer before seventh grade so that when we went trick-or-treating—dressed as a couple from the 1940s—she was a towering pinup in a thrift-store fur coat and I was her small beloved, swimming in her stepfather's naval dress uniform, my lip smudged with a mascara mustache. Abby, my tall Juliet. When a neighbor boy let us into an R-rated screening of *Shakespeare in Love,* we found we had the theater to ourselves and performed in the aisles, bowing, curtsying, reciting sonnets with the huge lips parting onscreen. It was a kind of love that was also mirroring.

One night in elementary school we stayed up to the witching hour and held hands in the dark. We were going to look into the black face of the vanity mirror on her dresser, we were going to confront something, but neither of us had the courage. We counted *one, two, three,* and then stared at each other instead, frightened of what we'd heard of eternity, how it cursed you. There were words we were supposed to recite, but we knew that just the eyes mattered, so closing them we walked blindly back to our sleeping bags, tripping on pillows until, lying down, we blinked them open at the chemical light of the glow-in-the-dark stars on her ceiling, still shining, late in the night.

Without a word, I feel her near to me. I bring her up like a strand of silver hair and a mirror. I could speak to her through the glass, but it's a trick of fog and reflection, just as deceptive as a camera and a filter. But I want to know how a body ages, how it grows, and the harder I look the more I see my bones rising to the surface. Maybe what we laid down then matters most of all. This rippling distorts even the simplest reflection.

HUNGER

The day before my wedding I was starving and surrounded by food. To keep within the slender lines of our budget, Joe and I had decided to make all the meals for our reception—dinner for 150 people—ourselves, here in the small kitchen of our rented house. It was July, and all week the temperature had risen over ninety degrees, with heavy clouds developing in the late afternoon, breaking open into brief, violent storms at sunset. When I woke early to start cooking, the world was wet and already hot. I found myself, alone in that small kitchen, cooking for a wedding that didn't feel like my own, too busy to eat or think twice about going through with it.

Joe wanted a pig roast, and, in his manner, which involved a bit of stealing and a bit of begging, he worked his way into a free pig from a farm north of us on the river. He wouldn't let me come with him to pick it up. *You wouldn't like it there, it's not your kind of place,* he said. Instead, he took his friend, Sven, a hulking mass of a man who was so tall I couldn't look him in the eyes. They picked up the pig in Sven's big truck and spent the better part of those two days poking at a fire and drinking New England moonshine made from fermented apples in Sven's backyard. They ate hot dogs and packs of gas station donuts, the same diet that sustained them when they sugared, fished, and hunted together, smoothed out by bowl after bowl of marijuana. When Joe came home those nights before the wedding he smelled of charcoal and over-sweet apples.

In preparation for all the cooking, I had the house set up like a storeroom, with dry goods on the kitchen table, platters on the couch, the fridge full of bulk goods, organized by dish. My recipes were printed and taped to the tile backsplash. I whipped butter with honey and formed butter flowers in small bowls, garnished with violets and nasturtiums. I sliced heirloom tomatoes, ruby and emerald gems, into thick slabs and dusted them with crystals of pink Himalayan salt. I massaged a lemon and maple vinaigrette into a flock of chicken breasts and seared them crispy over the grill. As I flipped the meat, I could look over the cornfield that stretched out to the river and over the hedge into the neat rows of the organic farm where I worked. Food was all around me, but I wasn't hungry. I forgot to eat. Nothing looked good.

What are you doing to yourself? The seamstress asked me during my final dress fitting. The white satin gown hung around my ribs. I stood with my arms raised like a scarecrow as she ducked under and around me, pinning up inches of loose fabric. *You can't lose any more weight,* she said, *you're already so tiny.* In the mirror, the dress became a shape, a body of its own. I didn't look like the woman I wanted to be. As soon as Joe proposed, I had begun altering myself, cleaning up my diet, working out. I scrubbed away at my face, soaked my hair in thick conditioners, oiled my nail beds at night, and drank hot lemon water, doing everything I could to change. I have never thought of myself as beautiful, but during that year, I wanted to shape-shift. I wanted to form a new self, a woman who fit into the story that my life was becoming. I thought if I could look like her, my image might bleed into hers. The wedding dress, with its final alterations, hung cool and slick in my closet, a new skin I might slip into and then, transform. Sometimes I snuck into the back room, where the dress was hidden, and ran my hands up it, hopefully.

The day before the wedding I didn't touch the dress. I hadn't even looked in on it. My hands were dirty and swollen in the humidity. Our battered air conditioning unit struggled against the oven's heat. My parents and sisters had offered to help, but I had declined, claiming to be a perfectionist. I told them it all had to be right, the grill marks on the chicken, the consistent slices of tomatoes, and the finely shredded strings of cabbage in the slaw. But it wasn't about getting it right. Cooking our wedding food was a ritual, a punishment for all the small choices—the *yeses* that should have been *nos*—that had led me to that place, between the hot stove and the cluttered counter, trapped because I didn't have to courage to be honest. I hoped the heat in the kitchen would purify me, like a sweat lodge, and I would be better for the long hours of work. I had taken the coward's route, decided to alter myself to fit the landscape of my life. And I was starving.

On the scale I weighed less than I had at age fifteen, less than I had weighed during my years of fad diets, of fasting and obsessive eating. I weighed more when I lived on the West Coast with a man who hated cooking and took me to the nicest restaurants in Los Angeles and Portland, Oregon. I weighed more when I lived in New Hampshire with a man who made his own kimchi, took shots of apple cider vinegar, and drank bottles of raw milk for lunch. Even when I lived on my own, eating a poor woman's diet of potatoes, oatmeal, and scrambled eggs, I was fuller, more graceful in the hip and thigh. The year before the wedding I lost everything. *Lean,* I called it, but it wasn't just a physical hunger, it was a deeper emptiness. I've read that people often get rid of their belongings prior to suicide. Before the wedding I cut away my dreams. One by one, like helium balloons, I let them go. I called it release, but it was starvation.

The night before my wedding I ate just one thing, a lemon sugar cookie frosted with royal icing and garnished with a sprig of lavender. I didn't think of it tasting good. The cookie had a good bake, was not overly sweet, and was firm on the bottom but still soft in the middle. I took my apron off and hung it over the door of the fridge. Upstairs, in my bathroom mirror, I looked at my face. My eyes were huge and dark. Despite my scrubbing, despite my visits to the cosmetologists and the hundreds of dollars in creams and washes she sold me, my forehead and jawline were still bumpy with acne. What she didn't tell me was that my body was reacting to stress, to hunger and depression, and that none of her designer creams or electric treatments could cure me. I needed a therapist, not a cosmetologist. Looking at myself I saw my bone structure, my collarbone as stark as a clothes hanger. I closed my eyes and pictured how I would be dressed the next day, the gown hanging off me, my face disguised by thick makeup and hidden by a veil. I hoped I would be beautiful and nothing like myself.

While I was in the bathroom I realized that I had forgotten to prepare one dish, a beet salad with caramelized red onions, walnuts, and chevre tossed with parsley and mint. There were logs of chevre in the fridge, bags of walnuts on the kitchen table, and bunches of herbs resting in mason jars on the counter, but no beets. I had to bake them that night because there wouldn't be time tomorrow to roast beets, between the hair appointments, the makeup application, and the reception setup. Joe was still at Sven's. I texted him, but he didn't reply. He often forgot to charge his phone. *Gone to the farm. Picking beets,* I wrote and looked into the bright screen of the phone, waiting. It went dark, and I slipped it into my back pocket.

The sun set under a mass of thunderheads in the west, bruising the eastern sky a deep purple. Wind knocked the leaves back and forth, and the white pine needles whooshed softly, like long sighs. The coming storm electrified the air, and birds called out from the bushes and hedges, chirping excited warnings. I parked my car at the farm and threw a few wax boxes in the back of the farm pickup. In the barn I walked through the dark, knowing by heart where to step to. Having worked there nearly half my life, I knew the land and its buildings—the barn, shed, and greenhouses—better than any other acres on earth. I dreamt, once, that the sun exploded, and I had to work the fields in complete darkness, but by touch and footfall I knew each turn in the road, each soft hill and rise of earth. The barn at night was full of memories that hung thick as braided garlic, full of oiled tools, stacked bushel baskets, boxes of ripe tomatoes, crates of seeds, and rows of rain boots. I grabbed a harvesting knife and ran the blade along the whetstone. Quick sparks flew, illuminating the worktable and the rough wood floors.

The truck I knew by memory too. The round head of the gearshift had been worn to fit my palm. The faint clutch sunk under my left foot; I knew how to play it like a pianist soft on the petals. The truck smelled of every person I had worked with, friends who were long gone, and also of rotting vegetables, tart green weeds, gasoline, WD-40, and metal. I rolled the windows down as I drove along the central road to the corner of the field by the riverbank to the biggest plantings of beets. Through cracks in the clouds, the western sky shone brightly, but the storm was a black thing that mounted the hills, moving quickly. Inside the clouds, lightning popped and sizzled, stretching like bright veins overhead. It made me shiver. A few years ago a kid on a neighboring farm had been struck and killed by lightning. After his death, I didn't let my crew work under storm clouds, no matter how distant, but the night before my wedding, I needed beets.

I harvested quickly, tossing the wax boxes down into the aisle. Bending over, with my legs locked, I ripped out handfuls of beets and lay them in piles. The storm rumbled. I realized that all the birds were quiet. Only the wind moving through the vegetable fields made any noise, wind through the thick broccoli plants and wispy fennel fronds, wind through the bold garlic and gentle lettuces and the big, red-veined leaves of the beets. Bending over I felt the thinness of my stomach, pulled up against my spine. I knelt down by the first pile and began cutting the beets from their leaves, stopping the knife against my thumb. Little beets, or beets that were split or soft, I threw away. This was all instinct, the cutting, the sorting; my body knew this work well. At the farm I could let my brain separate and move on its own, drifting through daydreams and memories.

I thought of a meal I had eaten in Portland, Oregon, at a hip restaurant called Clark Lewis in what was then a warehouse district. To get there I walked through train yards and abandoned industrial streets, carefully stepping, in my heels, over metal crates and potholes. I ordered ravioli stuffed with goat cheese and pink beets. Jason and I were celebrating something that night, I don't remember what. He might have gotten a piece published somewhere, or I could have reached a new mile record. I was training for a marathon and running further than I ever imagined. When I cut into the ravioli they were delightfully bright, like Barbie's dress, the sort of pink that smiles playfully. I remember when I ate them I could taste the sun in the cheese and the soil in the beets, and I told Jason this revelation, that in good food the whole world is visible. I marveled at the grass's ability to the turn the light of the sun into fuel for the goats and the goats' bodies to make sweet milk. I marveled at the seed in the soil, growing large on light, on rain, on nitrogen from lightning strikes and nutrients from the creation of the planet, chemicals deep in the ground. He laughed. We loved each other then. I cut a square off and passed it to him, and he closed his eyes and tried to imagine the hydrogen combustion in the sun, lightning, goats in a grassy pasture, and fields of sweet golden wheat. My lips were stained pink from the beets, a bright, happy lipstick.

The storm swept overhead and all the light in the western sky became blanketed by clouds. Across the field, I could see headlights pull into our driveway, and I knew that Joe was home. The headlights shut off and then the house lit up. I could see the windows over the corn. I wiped my hands on my thigh and checked my cellphone, but it remained silent. I rushed to the next pile, quickly cutting beets from greens. My heart pounding, I cut, tossed, cut, and tossed. Lightning jumped down upriver, and briefly I could see my red hands and my dirty knees. I pulled forward and cut through the last pile. The wind rolled through the fields wildly, rain started to fall, hitting the thick broccoli leaves and pinging off the hood of the truck. I wiped the knife off on my jean shorts and hauled the wax boxes full of beets to the truck bed. When I heaved them up I could tell how small I was, I could feel each muscle pulling and stretching. I had to use all my strength. For a moment I sat in the cab with the windows rolled up, watching the windshield run with rain. My stomach rolled, and I remembered that I hadn't eaten anything all day, just that one cookie. I told myself that when I got back to the kitchen, after I had washed, peeled, diced, and set the beets to roasting in the oven, I would eat something.

But when I returned, Joe was in front of the TV with his feet up on the ottoman, and I had nothing to say to him. He helped me carry in the beets and then sat back down. I tied the dirty apron around my waist and began to prepare the beets. While they were roasting, I chopped the walnuts in the food processor. Then I stripped mint and parsley and cut them into a fine green pile. On the stovetop, I added red onions to fry pans simmering with maple syrup and butter and stirred them until they were brown and translucent. I checked the beets and then turned the oven off. I'd let them cool in there overnight. Joe was asleep on the couch, in the corner that had formed to his shape. It was late, too late. I remembered that the makeup artist told me to get lots of sleep before the wedding, beauty rest, as she called it. My hands were stained red, red under my nails, red in my heartline and lifeline, red up to my wrists from beet juice. I ran them under hot water; I scrubbed at them with a nailbrush until they were pink and raw.

Under the shower, I washed them again. I stood beneath the stream and let it plaster my hair to my back and body. I looked down at my stomach drawn into my spine, my hipbones raised like a spoon's edge. At the end of the hunger, I thought there would be transformation, not just a thinner me but a better me. That was the myth that drove me. I've heard that the impulse to diet can start in the womb, and I imagined my mom, carrying me, all the while trying, as she always has, to loose ten pounds. Not a lot of weight, she'd say, just a few pounds. I used to go with her to Weight Watchers meetings and stand beside her as she weighed in. It wasn't just weight she wanted to lose, it was a bigger thing, a whittling down to find the better parts of herself, like under those few pounds a better woman waited to be revealed. I thought of Michelangelo searching the marble for the statue inside. In the shower, the water washed the cooking smells off me, the grill grease and tomato juice. I was thinner, but I wasn't better. Maybe, I thought, there was still more to lose, before, suddenly, I saw in the mirror that dream of myself transformed, a woman, confident in her beauty, light with grace and the authority of a life well lived. I could see her perfectly, I could almost reach out and touch this vision of myself, but there was hunger and darkness between us.

The night before the wedding I lay on my side of the bed curled toward the wall. The storm had passed, but the wind still scattered rain from the leaves outside, a wet, fresh sound. The house smelled delicious. I could pick out lemon, lavender, beets, grilled chicken, acidic tomatoes, honey, and syrup. I had forgotten to eat. The hunger had moved out of my stomach and seeped into my bones and chest, heavy as dark water. It was dense and throbbed like a bruise, and it made me aware of the voids in my body, my hollow stomach, and my empty heart. I'd had a dream, but I didn't remember. I never remembered my dreams then. I woke up the morning of my wedding hungry.

HEARTBEAT

Open to a church in rural Missouri. The glory of the place left years ago, packed up and headed west after some sunshine daydream. Now all that's left are peeling paint and a view out into spring fields where mud and sprout mix in a messy green. A skinny blond boy, too tall for his pleated polyester trousers, has taken a step out from the ranks of the choir toward the seated congregation. While the boy sings in a falsetto clear and cool as water from a seep, there isn't a soul who isn't drawn to him. In the front row, a farmer rings his rough hands together. A reek of alcohol sweats dark moons under his Sunday suit. A beautician, who, this very morning, has used her trade to conceal bruises on her cheek and wrist, smiles, and her mascara begins to run as tears fill her eyes. These are the boy's parents. This is not a movie. This is this boy's life.

Let's get to the heart of the story. In 1986 Don Johnson—an actor famous for playing the pastel-clad, swaggering cop from *Miami Vice* who made Armani shirts and Ray-Bans a veritable uniform for a certain type of eighties masculinity—decides to put out a rock album. Johnson has taught himself to play guitar, and he first learned to sing and perform in church. That life is a million acres of swamp, suburbia, and soy behind him now. He's put the work in, taken the acting classes, suffered nearly a decade of missed chances, and shacked up in a bungalow deep in the throat of Laurel Canyon with a fifteen-year-old Melanie Griffin whom he'll later marry and divorce twice. He's cultivated a history of significant drug and alcohol abuse. He's made friends, broken hearts, and no longer looks like the angelic blond kid who hacked his way out of the heartland to the California coast. Tanning, drugs, and sleepless nights have left him with the charmingly cut face of a playboy.

But Johnson is tired of all this. He's recently gotten sober; it's his nine-month-old son's eyes, he's said, not pleading but actually looking at him and seeing him for what he is. A guy stumbling sick into a dining room at dawn where a mother and child wait, like the Madonna and Christ, sunlit and milky before plates of shimmering grapefruit sections. As the clouds lift, he knows two things: he needs to stay sober and he wants to try something new, he wants to return to what first called him before a crowd. Don Johnson wants to make a hit rock and roll album.

He's written songs with the Allman Brothers and is friends with men who can make guitars scream like his female fans on Wall Street, who, while he was filming an episode of *Miami Vice,* showered their panties down from office building windows onto the heads of Johnson and his costar, Philip Michael Thomas (shooting had to be delayed while some poor tech, hopefully dressed in surgical-grade latex, picked up all those high-cut thongs). Tom Petty, Dickey Betts, Stevie Ray Vaughn, Ronnie Wood, Willie Nelson, and Dweezil Zappa all sign on to Johnson's album, a posse of talent.

"I wanted the record to be modern, tough rock," Johnson told the *LA Times* when the album first dropped, "I didn't want it to sound like something that other people designed and I just stopped by for a few minutes to do the vocals. And I made it clear that I would walk away from it if I didn't think it was credible." But what Johnson delivers is the uncanny valley of rock and roll. "Heartbreak" is the cancerous aspartame to the straight-up sugar that Nelson, Stevie Ray Vaughn,

Petty, the Rolling Stones, and Zappa shot straight up the nostrils of listeners like toddler beauty pageant queens blowing pixie sticks.

The title track given to Johnson by his producer is a song written for Helen Reddy, famous for her seventies feminist anthem "I Am Woman." It sank to the bottom of one of her albums and was never released as a single. Perhaps it was with humor that someone pitched the song for Johnson, the Poseidon of Panties, but either way, in 1986 Johnson says the lyrics reflected his relationship with his ex-wife and beloved son—the owl-eyed kid who had sobered him up. How the confusion of words meant anything to him—for instance, how anyone could look for something that was a sound, or what a person without a heartbeat could feel other than dead—is a mystery. Maybe Johnson knows that a little mystery, like a five o'clock shadow, isn't always a bad thing. He won't reveal the names of his first two wives, but you can easily find his naked butt cheeks in a 1979 *Playboy* spread. It's a matter of image, after all. The marriages were embarrassments, one-day flings in college in Kansas and on the set of his first movie. He reinvents. He's a club kid. He's at the Factory with Warhol, he's posing nude with his famous girlfriend. Now, deep into the excess of *Miami Vice* success, *Rolling Stone* magazine writes "Don Johnson Wants to Be a Rock and Roll Star." It's bad when what you want, rather than what you are, makes the headline.

"Heartbeat," the title song on the album, climbed to number five on the Billboard charts and even higher on German and Austrian lists, a calculation that music theorists might one day discover to be essential to the determination of bad songs. It was the age of MTV, and thus it was proclaimed that every song must have its music video. So an entire concept video album was assembled in which Johnson staggered, with uncomfortable sincerity, through dramatized romances and stages that look like tic-tac-toe boards. He's too handsome to be a rock star and too vulnerably average as a singer to bear the emotional weight required to raise up nonsense lyrics. The result is something like an album made by a fictional character in the style of the era: a mid-1980s version of the Monkees, where, instead of innovating or collaborating, Johnson settles instead for a tragic bid at credibility. Looking like you're trying hard to fit in is the antitheses of rock and roll.

What we all love is the original story, a simple pattern of rise and fall and flatline. It's 2004, and I'm on the roof of a hotel, twenty-five stories above the shimmering obsidian tarmac of the Miami airport. Underage, I've been drinking out of the adults' discarded glasses at a gala to celebrate young artists, to celebrate me. I have danced with Robert Redford's business partner, and he's told me how panthers scream in the jungle. Now on the roof of the hotel, there's a box of Domino's pizza and my friend Max, leaning against the cement wall of the stairwell, and above us the bellies of jets dip so low they take all the sound with them. They scream over the needle tip of a flagpole flying the stars and stripes.

I shout Hunter S. Thompson quotes at the planes like a kid throwing rocks at the water. "When the going gets weird, the weird turn professional!" I shout. "Freedom is something that dies unless it's used." But the words only ripple in my head. I want to take the flag down and wear it as a cape, wrapped around my pulsing, sunburnt skin.

It's a late afternoon in Woody Creek, Colorado. Don Johnson and Hunter S. Thompson are sitting in Johnson's garage among all the muscle cars of his private collection, the hoods sleek as jungle cats. Through the open door, they can see Owl Range, where Thompson blows up Jeeps and rides his lawn tractor in a bathrobe, and where, just a few years from this afternoon, he ends his life with a bullet to the brain. Thompson has a sloshing highball of whiskey and is smoking through a gold-tipped cigarette holder. Johnson is smoking, too, but drinking nothing. He hasn't had a drink in a decade, but he still loves the heat of the Gonzo journalist. They talk racing, boats, and cars. They talk a new show into life, they write together in dogged afternoon sessions before Thompson spills over the brink of toxicity. They call it *Nash Bridges* after the title character, and it's an inside joke that grows into another hit for Johnson.

Thompson is getting sloppy, and Johnson starts to tease him. The writer has recently completed an online course in Zen, and Johnson asks him a riddle.

"What is the sound of one hand clapping?" Faced with a traditional koan, something to be mulled over, the Gonzo man doesn't need time, he's electric with ideas. Moving both the cigarette holder and the high ball glass into his left hand, he swings his open palm and slaps Johnson full across his handsome face. Johnson's ears begin to ring as if someone has discharged a handgun near his head.

"That's the sound of one hand clapping," Thompson says.

Johnson's ears ring for days and days.

In the music video for "Heartbeat," Johnson is trapped in a dark box of a room, bumping into listless dancers. He wails to the floor; he screams to the echoing blackness of the soundstage. A sixteen-year-old Dweezil Zappa plays the guitar uncomfortably close to Johnson, like a kid trying to piss off their parent. Johnson stares straight ahead and, getting no reaction, Zappa drifts into the middle of the tic-tac-toe board of the stage. No one, not the dancers, not the flat-lined band, pays Johnson any attention. His intensity played against the delirious coolness of the musicians makes his performance as an actor even more apparent.

Outside, in the dramatic narrative of the movie, Johnson has cut the sleeves off nearly every item of his clothing save for his signature Armani tank tops, which are already sleeveless. The Chrysler Building looms like some monolith of meaning, but it's the only indicator we'll get for the rest of the movie that it's taking place in the real world. While filming a swarming protest on the streets, a passing super model catches Johnson's eye, and then she's gone. He looks for her in some unspecified tropical village where she appears first posing for a photoshoot on the hood of a burning car and again while slipping a black mask over her face—is she part of the resistance? A ninja? A Wild West bank robber? Taking health precautions?

Back in his studio, assisted by Paul Shaffer in a jolting celebrity cameo, Johnson sorts through all of his footage for the image of this perfect woman, flipping through his war photos for a shot of a hot babe. The badness of this narrative, ignoring the world and focusing solely on a singular object of desire, is matched only by the badness of the lyrics, which seem to break Johnson's voice to pieces at the end, grinding his vocal chords by weight of sheer repetition. The only moment in which Johnson realizes the quest in the song is when he looks up at the word *Heartbeat* pulsing across a building in branded neon.

This frantic search for life, looking for a heartbeat in the streets, is the ridiculous task of a limited gaze. There is nothing inherently wrong about wanting something badly, hunger mixed with talent under the crucible of training and work ethic should forge something resembling art, but what makes "Heartbeat" so heartbreaking is the terrible self-awareness of Johnson. No one is helping him solve this riddle. Clearly, the world is full of heartbeats, the rhythms of blood through the body and the earth are our earliest and most universal drumlines.

Scientists have determined that everything with a heart is given about one million beats. Humans, due to their exceptionally long periods of childhood and adolescence, which slow the cell's aging process, are the outliers in the mammal kingdom. We've got two and a half million beats to work with. This is an average of course, true to the species but not the individual, which means that some will beat much more and some much less than others. Small animals, like the Etruscan shrew, have hearts that skitter out 835 beats per minute. A blue whale, whose heart is the size of a Prius and whose arteries are large enough for a human to walk through upright, can slow its heart rate to three beats per minute while diving hungry into the depths. Hearts beat slower as they age, too, an infant's faster than a grandma's, a woman's always slightly faster than a man's. Nearly every living creature—save for the oddities of jellyfish, sea cucumbers, and corals—have hearts, and those hearts beat in a rhythm prescribed to them through the ages. Even the earth beats, twofold. Beneath our feet magma pulses in the deep time of geology, and above us, electromagnetic fields—generated and excited by lightning discharges—resonate at exactly 7.83 Hz.

A heartbeat is not hard to find. The first sound all womb-born mammals hear is the pulse of blood through their mother's body, amplified by the ocean of fluids they float in. Who hasn't marveled at the sound in a lover's chest, when, ear to breastplate, you listened as the miniature rivers of the body moved perfectly, this great beautiful mechanism, this animated mystery? Love, of course, and art, are collective experiences of awakening, their discovery being the awareness of the complexity and glory of the universe.

I am back in Miami, not a native or even a tourist. My work with the same art program I attended as a teenager puts me up on the twenty-first floor of a corporate hotel and sends me off to campus daily on a ten-minute walk inland as part of the creative writing team. At dawn or dusk, I run small explorations, two miles, three miles, out and back from the hotel through streets and over the Venetian Causeway, past Star

Island, where Don Johnson used to live, commuting by speed boat to the set of *Miami Vice*. The buildings are the color of French candy, and the cars roar in Italian. The wind slaps the bay against the seawall and palms shuffle like tarot cards on their strange bird legs. Here, the police look like dancers. Some tailor has been working hard to cut those uniforms tight around each set of toned glutes and wide-winged lats. At dusk, thunderheads ride the uplift at the coast, turning their beautiful, bruised profiles inland.

Most reviews of Johnson in *Miami Vice* said that his years of drugs and partying produced an authentic performance. It's common to find praise for all sorts of addictive behavior in relation to works of art. This assumption of experience as authenticity has become the root of an ongoing dialogue this week. I want it to be spoken about carefully, because what I heard, at the age of the young writers in my group, was a recipe for substance abuse. Addiction seemed like a readymade code, a stand-in for the artistic life. Of course, genetic markers beating through my heart helped too. My father warned us of this growing up. I was so sheltered by his moderation that it was easy to reject, like I rejected everything else, friendship, advice, commitment, responsibility. I spent decades looking for the obvious things that my addiction concealed.

The story of addiction is true to the group, not always to the individual. To write one does not have to escape the body, to slip skins, to transfuse blood—this appropriation of form, this character acting is the root of much of the group's discussion. The creative team, myself included, are reminded that two years ago we worked through the aftermath of the Parkland shootings and the ripple of the Pulse nightclub attack upcoast. We begin to make a list as a group: hurricanes, shootings, floods. The students are steeped in these traumas. Still, they are careful about who gets to tell what story. We look at each other, back and forth, across conference tables, lunch tables, bus seats, paving stones, the question beating like a heart between us, story and speaker.

The curse of the addict is the constant mirror gaze of self-reflection, the ringing in the ears that last for days. Myself in this chair writing. Johnson outside his home on Star Island having his picture taken for an article about "Heartbeat" that will run in the *LA Times*. The photographer suggests something musical to add to the authenticity of the scene. Johnson replies that he owns a prized guitar, a gift from the Allman Brothers, but no, he doesn't want to hold it. That's not right. Johnson posing, aware of how he looks and how the picture will make him look, shrugging off the guitar, talking to his son on the phone, eating pasta salad by the gleam of Biscayne Bay, watching himself from outside himself. When *Rolling Stone* comes to interview him, Johnson changes his mind about the guitar. The picture runs inside the cover article "Don Johnson Wants to Be a Rock and Roll Star" and it looks exactly as he worried it would. A movie star posed with a prop.

For a day in Miami, the young writers and their creative team are locked in rehearsal in a small theater. The performance is in the evening, and the small space will be packed with wealthy patrons, teachers, parents, and the other art area winners. The stage is a twenty-four-square-foot box set in front of black curtains and surrounded on three sides by rows of chairs. It looks like the set of "Heartbeat," black disappearing into universal emptiness under the blind of the stage lights.

The writers are reluctant as a group to dance as they deliver the final, joint lines of a collaborative piece they've written. The director wants them to sway over to the piano where the classical musicians will riff off a solemn piece the tuba player composed as a tribute to the Parkland victims, transitioning, chord by chord, into a Mardi Gras-style funeral march, a dirge that is also a dance to celebrate the dead. The writers, who are prouder of their words than their physicality, don't want to be viewed by their peers as awkward. They are worried about what the graceful ballerinas will see when they look at the writers, with scripts in their hands, trying to find a beat. Hell, even the theater kids can dance!

With only a few hours to curtain, the creative team tells the writers that they need to collaborate and find a solution. Their plan is twofold—one: they'll do their best, but they won't fake it; and two: they'll text their friends who will be in the audience and ask them, if the spirit moves them, to rise from their seats at the end of the show and dance out on stage. The proximity of the audience allows for this breaking of the wall.

You know how this song works. You can see it coming from a mile away, a lumbering, simplified creature, as exposed as the heart is hidden. It took centuries of violating the dead and torturing the living for scientists to understand that most central of organs. Typically, healthy hearts make only two audible sounds. The first heart sound is described as a *lub,* and the second is called *dub.* A physician listening with a stethoscope can hear the two distinct sounds of the heartbeat but can only see them, as Johnson sings, if an EKG machine is set up to monitor the heart. And then it's not hard to look for at all; it's a blinking screen, just off to the side. Asystole is the complete absence of any detectable electrical activity of the heart muscle. It appears as a flat line on the monitors of an EKG machine, and what it feels like without a heartbeat is most certainly the end of life as you know it.

The switch from looking for a heartbeat to asking what it feels like without one is not the turn you hoped for. There's no coming back now. You don't expect the song to go there, but it does, so repetitive as to become mystical. Suddenly we are talking about the dead, or we are in love with the dead, or we are all just in this song together, trying to break out of the final lines, which are repeated more than a dozen times.

In the last scene, the night is coming to an end. At the finale of the show, the writers fold their scripts and shimmy over to the gleaming hood of the concert piano. They eye each other nervously, hoping to be collective in their awkwardness. They begin to sway, and the music rises, the tuba pulsing and the drums beating. The polite violinist yields to the melody, her hair falling over her instrument, and the whole audience stands, cheering, unbelieving, as every young artist rises from their seats and joins their peers onstage, forming a dance line that absorbs the writers and encircles the musicians. Clapping becomes a drumline, a sound playing into and beneath the music. The circle forms fully, linked with nearly a hundred bodies on stage, pulsing around the musicians. The dancers jump into the center, break dancing, leaping, hip-hop, ballet, and tap. The beat is easy to find, in the blood and in the palms, and we're all holding the same simple rhythm—two sounds, silence and noise—and at the moment, nobody is trying to be anything other than part of that collective, authentic heartbeat.

ON RUNNING

I want to say up front that I am not a good runner. I am neither very fast nor very graceful. I don't run competitively, although I have completed a few races. But nor am I a jogger. Some people would tell you that running is a movement at over six miles per hour while jogging takes place at a slower speed; in both gaits, there is a moment when both feet are off the ground. Some people would tell you that runners strike the earth with the forefoot while joggers strike with their heels, but in fact, many competitive long-distance runners are heel strikers. For me, the difference between the two comes down to intent. Jogging is something like a shuffle, a lack of commitment to intensity. But running . . . running is a pursuit or an escape. To run, the body goes all in; every ligament and muscle fiber strikes, pulls, and returns to the earth; the runner tips forward like the front edge of a wheel, rolling into space.

I remember the first time I ran. I felt like a queen, divine on the earth. I was thirteen, and I had never run before. I remember the night clearly because of its novelty and because running is a little like taking flight. I often dream that if I run fast enough I will begin to fly, as if speed on the runway is all the jet plane requires.

* * *

PACE

Noun

1. A walking step, not too long, not too short—in the US, roughly two and a half feet.

The sort of step I take around the edge of my yard in the morning, surveying the quality of the coming day.

Verb

1. To walk at a steady rate, back and forth, as an expression of anxiety.

2. To keep pace.

3. To measure by walking.

To pace is both to lead and establish competitive speed and to do something slowly in order to prevent overexerting. That is, although John Henry kept pace with that steam engine, he did not pace himself, and his heart burst; flooded rivers of blood ran out while the cold steel kept ringing.

* * *

In my sixth-grade history class, we did research papers on famous explorers. I was assigned Lewis and Clark and the Corps of Discovery. I became enamored of the two captains (although Clark was never officially granted that title) and especially fond of Lewis, who seemed, even from my amateur research in the middle school's library, to be somewhat eccentric, somehow unfitting of the explorer archetype. Lewis was prone to what his contemporaries, including Thomas Jefferson, described as "hypochondria," noting that the condition ran in his family. Modern medicine would see him diagnosed with severe depression.

In 1809, at the age of thirty-five, Lewis died by suicide. It had been three years since the expedition had returned to St. Louis. In that time, he had run up debts, developed a crippling addiction to alcohol, struggled at his post as governor of the

Upper Louisiana Territory, failed at love, and been unable, or perhaps simply too depressed, to complete his written account of his great journey. He was carrying the manuscript with him when he died. Revisionist biographers claim that his death was murder, noting the brutal nature of his killing. Even as a girl, I knew this was wistful, their need to rewrite a hero's end.

I include the details of that night here only to summon the horror I felt as a girl at the absolute darkness of suicide, that shutdown of all possible routes. First, according to the coroner's report, a gunshot wound to the head, then another to the chest, neither fatal, fired from his pistols. When Lewis's servants found him, he was slumped in his buffalo and bearskin robes, slicing his veins from elbow to wrist with his shaving razor. He begged his men to take his rifle and blow out his brains; he told them they could have all the money in his trunk for that service. He asked them for water. "It is so hard to die," he is reported to have said. Alone in the wilderness, his men tried to patch him up, they spooned water to his lips. He bled out before dawn.

"I fear the weight of his mind has overcome him," Clark wrote to Thomas Jefferson, notifying him of Lewis's passing. A few months prior to Lewis's death, Clark had named his first son Meriwether Lewis Clark. He didn't know that, during the final drunk, hallucinatory days of Lewis's life, his former traveling companion claimed constantly that Clark was near and would help him. His servant reported him saying that "he herd [sic] Clark coming on, and Said that he was certain we would over take him, that he had herd of his Situation and would Come to his releaf." I thought of the times when the two had separated on their journey to pursue forked waterways or explore passes through the mountains, and how easily, and with what faith, they had found each other again in the wilderness. At his most lost, Lewis had reached for Clark to locate him.

I wrote a research paper from the point of view of Lewis before he fired the first bullet, in a series of educational flash-backs. To me, he became a symbol of discovery, of expansion, but also of emptiness. How, I wondered—and wonder still— could a man fill his memories with so many maps of beauty, herds of ten thousand buffalo, Indian ponies in the Bitter-roots, the Great Falls of the Missouri, and still shut down that vision from within?

Could you run fast enough, or far enough, to escape your-self? I think not. I think Lewis taught me that you can't out-run yourself.

* * *

When I was five years old, I almost died from a lack of oxy-gen. It felt not so much like Darth Vader's invisible hand stran-gling my throat as like a slow march away from light. My nail beds turned blue. So did my lips. In the hospital, as my blood was being drawn and a mask slipped over my face connecting me to breathing machines, I remember the sensation of tun-nel vision, zooming in on the flooring tiles. By the time I got to the hospital, the scary part, the "I can't breathe" part, was long past. Sometime in that breathless night I had come to terms with the fact that I could die, though I think I must have understood it only as not breathing. I might have said that I understood that I could stop breathing and then rest, for it is very hard to breathe into the tight fist of asthmatic lungs, and I had been fighting that constriction for hours. The long sleep of death would have been welcome.

And because I had learned that it was actually rather easy to die, after I recovered from that near-fatal attack, death became even more frightful. Death was in every inhale, every game of tag, every hide-and-go-seek chase, every gym class. My asthma was triggered by allergens and temperature changes, so petting a cat could be deadly, or helping my dad mow the lawn, or waiting outside in a frigid New England winter for school to begin and then charging into an overheated room in my snowsuit.

My childhood was a well-regulated series of interactions, aided by medications. In any other era, I would surely have died, if not on that night when I was five, then on one of the many other occasions when even triple doses of inhaled steroids failed and I was rushed to the ER. The doctors said there was a chance I might outgrow it entirely, but to imagine that I could grow out of such a routine, that my lungs would change like my breasts and hips, seemed impossible.

* * *

Dear Meriwether Lewis,

In your dreams the country becomes a map with waterways like a surgeon's guide to the circulatory system, upcountry, downstream, all following the easiest path. The mountains rise and again you are trapped in the snowy gulches and deep-throated avalanche channels. You at the mouth of the Columbia, where I've read there are more waterfalls than anywhere else in the world; great corridors fall down into that river, steep and tough in the north and choked with a mist that breaks through the spruce and cedar at the coast. You are there at the edge of everything, camped for the wet season in a shingled fort, the rain in your bones and in the blue of your wrist veins. You trace them up the forearm, to that soft spot in the elbow, and then up through your shoulder and across the breastbone, to where they meet and pulse. There is nothing to do but return, with your bags filled with specimens, the shining birds and prairie creatures, gutted and eyeless.

* * *

When Thomas Jefferson wrote the King of Spain and asked if he might send a party into their territory for the purpose of "literary pursuits," he meant to increase geographic and scientific knowledge.

When Jefferson wrote in his rough draft of the Declaration of Independence, "We hold these truths to be sacred & undeniable; that all men are created equal & independent, that from that equal creation they derive rights inherent & inalienable, among which are the preservation of life, & liberty, & the pursuit of happiness," he didn't mean happiness in the modern sense. The root of that word implies fortune, luck that was once associated with the whim of the gods. Jefferson meant this older form of happiness, the happiness of the ancient writers, like Cicero and Plato, for whom it was found through morality, justice, and duty. Cicero wrote that "a happy life consists in tranquility of the mind." That tranquility consisted of living virtuously.

When the assassins hired by Mark Antony finally caught up to a fleeing Cicero on the road outside of Rome, they found the old essayist sweating in his carriage.

Accepting his fate with manly grace, Cicero bared his throat to his murderers like a defeated gladiator. Once the orator's body was brought to Rome, Antony ordered the hands and head to be cut off, and he had them displayed on the Rostrum in the Forum where Cicero had once delivered his famous speeches. The hands brutalized for having written those words. His head defiled for having spoken them. Antony's wife pulled out Cicero's tongue and jabbed it with her hairpin, so bitterly did she hate his essays against her husband's power.

When you say *happiness* think of a hairpin in the tongue and imagine fleeing for your life on a cedar-lined road, smell the dust and the horses. When you say *freedom* think of a life of essays. When you say *power* imagine two old hands.

* * *

YARD

Noun

1. The length of a man's belt in medieval England. Irked by the inconsistency of his countrymen's middles, King Henry I measured the distance between his nose and the thumb of his outstretched hand and standardized the unit.

In a Chinese-food restaurant, I once overheard the combustion of a first date as a drunk woodworking teacher explained to a stone-faced woman that he forced his students to use his body's measurements to make their pencil boxes and birdhouses. "One Bob!" he called it and held his foot up for her so she could take note of that exact unit. The woman shuddered. Only kings can get away with this sort of thing.

To measure the world with one's body seems a particularly gross form of egotism. But who understands time and distance in theory alone and not through the measurement of individual days or steps along a familiar running path?

* * *

I am in the pinewoods, and the light is still golden like it is in the summer in Maine. I am in my girl body again, lighter and strange to me. It is a body I have just been given, and it seems to do things on its own as if it just became mortal. We are playing capture the flag. The ground is a soft golden carpet of fallen needles.

The light is behind me. I feel its last warmth on my shoulder blades. At first, I am walking. I leap to cross a log, and then I leap to cross another, and then I am running. I am not playing, I am not running for a flag, I am running for movement. Oh, the ground is soft under my sneakers! And the light fades behind me so that I am running into the darkness of the woods, and the sound of the other girls is getting dim behind me, and I am up a slight hill, and still running, and my legs move like some animal's, and my arms pump like strong pistons. I breathe in through my mouth and nose and then out again clear and fleshy, almost bloody but healthy, like the taste of a coin.

I run and leap until I am high up where the ground gives way to boulders, the bones of Maine, and I look down and see the lake and the camp's roofs and docks. The girls yip in the pinewoods like coyotes, and briefly I feel myself above everything, the systems in my body working invisible and perfect, pulsing, exchanging, and I love it for the first time ever, this body that is now mine, but night is close, so I head back. Running down is almost better than running up. I am pumping and swift, and sweat is rising then running its own course over me, salty and new, until I am again among the girls from my cabin, and they are sweaty, too, and out of breath, and we walk together under the flickering streetlights down the sandy path to our bunks.

I could measure my life in the running trails I have followed. I could map it for you—from that first evening to this morning when I returned to my home, flushed with sweat, and after closing my pores with a cold shower, sat down to essay running, to measure it properly against what I know of myself.

In 2007, when I lived in Portland, Oregon, I visited Cape Disappointment and Fort Clatsop. During the stay of the Corps of Discovery it was a miserable place; now it's transformed into an educational national memorial. The replica of Lewis and Clark's split-log fort has been lacquered a shiny honey gold, and costumed rangers lead groups from the gift store to the film hall. The day I went, it was sunny, and the spruce needles glistened underfoot. Later, I drove along the Columbia River, marveling at the power of the water and the height of the gorge walls. All along the rocks, tiny waterfalls drained into the mighty river. I imagined Lewis shivering on the coast, bored during the cold, rainy winters. "Everything moves on in the old way," he wrote—a haunting description of cabin fever.

At the time I was training for my first marathon, and I took my long runs on Sauvie Island, just north of the city, where the Wilmette River joins the Columbia. Lewis and Clark camped there, ate a potato-like food that grew wild on the island, and then pushed back upstream toward the mountains. As I ran, I imagined I was retracing their routes, expanding their maps each night. The long runs took up three or four hours of my Sunday, and I was always flush with excitement beforehand, wondering what I might see on the road. The running mind is the traveling mind, noting each odd color, granting each license plate and cloud formation significance. I gave names secretly to houses and trees I passed, just as Lewis gave his own names to rivers and mountains.

* * *

Foot
Noun
1. The average length of a man's foot.
A woman's foot is smaller, which is not to say her world is smaller but rather measured differently. My foot is nine inches long.

* * *

In 2007, when I was twenty-two, I purchased a how-to book that began with the reassuring sentence, "Oprah ran a four-hour marathon." The book was slim and contained training plans. It divided the work of training for a marathon into three categories: the long run, once a week, which I would take on Sauvie Island; the short run, which I would loop around my apartment complex; and sprint intervals, which I would complete under the lights on my college's track, long after the sports teams had left the field for the night. The long runs I found to be an exercise in patience. My mind created its own tricks, calculating my speed, naming the houses and farms I passed, watching the mountains on the horizon as Lewis and Clark might have as they rowed up the Columbia. The short weekday runs of between two and five miles were charmingly repetitive, in the sense that I could depart with no expectation for a timed mile. Fitting them in was the challenge since I could generate only a little enthusiasm for the slog. The track workouts, which consisted of quarter-mile sprints followed by prescribed rest periods, were the most physically demanding portion of my training. One loop around the track accounted for a quarter mile, so I could mark my pace easily. The struggle was to stay steady from start to finish, to push through with my original thrust during the final one hundred meters.

My lungs burned. My legs threw themselves long on the track's surface. The bright white lights above the fields made me feel Olympic, although I was alone in the drizzle and dusk. During the minutes of rest, my ragged breath seemed amplified, all-consuming. Sweat grew cool on my skin. Then, at the beep of my watch's timer, I was off again, along the same path, trying to summon the drive forward with all my body calling for speed. The sprint required, in a short period, many cycles of motivation, like a compression of many days into one intense hour. Each sprint was its own expedition around the track, past the bleachers, the lampposts, the stadium gates. Every time I broke free from the starting line I had to commit, again, to flight.

* * *

To understand why I run, know that I both love and hate my body and have come to accept this balancing act. My body is like blood, constantly in flux, sometimes depleted and sometimes new and full of life. My body has been sick, and my spirit has hated being in a sick body. And of course I wish my body was something that it isn't. I wish it were taller and longer. I wish my neck would grow a few inches and that my shoulders weren't as wide as my hips. I could go on. When I was a sick kid, I dreamed of waking up in a new body. I dreamed of flying.

But when I am running, I must be with the body I have. Love it or hate it, there is no escape from it. Under the discipline of miles, the virtue of routine is that there is no turning back. There is just forward motion—feet pulling, hip flexors sweeping my legs back, my arms swinging, my chest slightly forward, trying to breathe and not swallow the wind. The violence of running fills my body. Even at my leanest, running shakes me loose. Fatty female hips and ass jiggle, and I feel heavier than when I am standing still, as if motion itself increased gravity. I feel my bad right knee and my tight left hamstring and the curve in my spine where scoliosis takes it off course before it veers back again. There is no hiding when I am running.

To make it to the road I must first inhale medication, so before I even set out, I acknowledge my limitations. *This*, my body screams, *is what you've got!*

* * *

HORSEPOWER

Noun

1. The amount of power required to lift seventy-five kilograms one meter in one second.

The engineer James Watt, who designed the machines that dug the coal that fed England's Industrial Revolution, calculated that a horse could turn a mill wheel 144 times an hour. He sold his steam engines on the power of the horse. Imagine all those beasts pulling, their breath rising, their hides slick—imagine that power inside a steel piston.

Everyone then had seen how hard a horse can work. Now, no one can remember it.

An article in *Nature* cites measurements from the 1926 Iowa State Fair reporting the peak output of show horses at 14.9 horsepower (which lasted but a brief few seconds as they pulled a weighted sled through damp sand in the humidity of a late August evening).

Many years later, on a cool August night in Berlin, under the flickering lights of the Olympiastadion's half-domed ceiling, Usain Bolt generated just 3.5 horsepower during the 9.58 seconds it took him to run a hundred meters, which was faster than any other recorded man or woman. No holding back, no! He wins! He kept running after crossing the finish line, at least another hundred meters, first holding his pointer fingers out long like a conductor orchestrating the cheering crowd, then with his arms out wide like wings.

* * *

Whenever I move to a new place, or vacation somewhere for more than a few days, one of the first things I do is to go for a run. I am, like most, a creature of habit, so when I find a route that is enjoyable—a good length with varying terrain, not too many cars, no scary places like dark tunnels or alley-ways where I might meet my end, and interesting things to look at; ideally a loop, but if not, then an out and back—I run it again and again until I start to read the landscape for markers of my pace, until I start to tell the same story again and again.

* * *

Dear Meriwether Lewis,

In the history books, they show you on a rise above the plains, in leather and uniform with a breeze from the Continental Divide blowing the fringe on your jacket back toward the Missouri. You squint into the western sun, like some great bird, just ahead of Clark with his sunburned skin and heavy forearms. I have always imagined you right before you put the first bullet in your head. Your intake of breath like the storms first tracking up valley, your eyes closed, finding your temple with the gun barrel, setting your teeth, and outside in that trailside inn, the other people drinking and falling asleep without terror and the country filling in all the places that were only prairies and mountain ranges in your maps and all of their quick starts at the sound of the gun while you faded, backward through increasing darkness, up to the spring source where the purest water rises.

* * *

"Have you reckoned the earth much?" asks Whitman. If you have run the same route many times, I think you have—at least that piece of it. You've learned its terrain, its highs and lows. You are familiar with its smells during different seasons and times of days (the sweet grass of summer, the dull salt of winter, the rising, swampy springtime mornings, and the sharp autumn sunsets). You know the pattern of traffic and the paths of animals. On the side of the road you find the things that happened when you weren't there to notice. During the night, deer were hit, trash was thrown, a bottle was broken over the blacktop. On each run a new note reveals itself. Two fence posts closer together than all the rest. A tree scarred by a snowplow. On a clear, sunny day in November, when all the leaves are down, you look further into the woods and notice an old shack by the creek. The body works hard here on the hill but not on the long downslope to the pasture. And here the road tilts to prevent flooding and your ankles sway under that strain. Jump a puddle. Skip over a rock that has rolled down from the cliff. Here the blood pulsing hard in the ears. Here the sweat drying on your cheeks. Here the howls of dogs. Here a strange silence from the swamp, the half-built subdivision, the echoing farmland.

* * *

Acre

Noun

1. The amount of land an ox can till in a day.

Like a man-hour, this unit is subject to specific conditions: the ox, the driver (a man of tolerance? A man of violent need?), the soil, the air through which they both must push.

The bones in our feet shifted as we began to walk upright. The shape of a foot can date a skeleton as quickly as a skull or jaw. As we evolved, the opposable big toe was phased out so that we can no longer hang from a branch with our feet as we can grip a barbell or bike handle or steering wheel with our hands. We became runners. We didn't evolve to escape from lunging lions or packs of dire wolves; humans aren't great sprinters. And anyway, everyone knows running from predators is a bad idea; not only will it trigger their drive to chase, but we simply can't win that race. Instead, ancient humans were long-distance runners; they pursued animals until they ran up against cliffs or fell shaking to the earth with capture myopathy. In this hunt our hairlessness was perhaps our greatest advantage. We could sweat and release heat while our furry prey overheated to its death, and in this manner a beast with two legs could catch a beast with four.

* * *

There are traditional running cultures, and I claim no connection to their practices. When I think of the Tarahumara of Mexico or the Kalenjin people of the African plains, I think always of my own death. I simply could not have survived in any time other than this one, and so nostalgic daydreams of living and running in times past are not longings of mine. I run to stay in shape, a problem that my ancestors would not have understood, in the same way that I can't imagine the power of a horse on a mill wheel. What haunts me is the idea of the chase, followed by the idea of escape, and the concept of measuring the earth with a body.

I have run away since I was a little girl, packing up and leaving home, moving instead of fighting. I have a powerful flight instinct. I say I run in pursuit of health, but I am also escaping its opposite. The idea of fitness is as powerful to me as my fear of sickness. My asthma is not influenced by my running, but my running will always be influenced by my asthma. The two exist together but are not equally affected. I will never outrun my asthma, but it will always bear on my running.

Through the map of years, they hunt each other. One winning. One retreating, then charging back. There are seasons when I am invincible. There are days when I come into my body weeping for its weakness. But had I nothing to fight against, perhaps I'd have nothing to pursue.

* * *

Every clear night of their journey Lewis and Clark made celestial observations, sometimes staying up well after their men, reworking their complex implements. On cloudy nights, when there were no visible stars to cast onto, they noted the temperature and tended to their maps. Even on days when neither man wrote a journal entry, they entered information on longitude, latitude, temperature, and weather. They named the rivers and mountains they'd passed during the day after sweethearts, heroes, and the virtues of the Masonic order. Although their collected work fills volumes, it is still incomplete. Whole books were lost or, perhaps, never existed. For instance, there are only two entries made by Lewis during the first push of their journey up the Missouri. Clark dutifully kept a log, but Lewis—who spent his days walking the banks alongside the Corps' small fleet of boats, botanizing and keeping an eye out for the Sioux—expressed his thoughts on paper only twice during this period. Was he joyous beyond words? Was he so focused on his saturated vision of expansion that the overflow of ink onto paper seemed unnecessary? He left to Clark the task of journaling, and I imagine him on the banks of the Missouri in the early fall of 1804, drawn away as intensely by happiness as he would later be isolated by pain.

The following spring, after the party pushed off from Fort Mandan and rounded the great bend of the Missouri, Lewis's journal entries thicken. Some are over five thousand words long and would have taken him, at a stream-of-consciousness pace, about two hours to write. He seemed to have words for everything: specimens, geography, bear encounters. It's during this time that he produced his best travel writing, summoning a sense of adventure and grandeur in his prose. But on June 13, walking ahead of the party as he often did, he confronted a sight that, despite his many words, he felt unprepared to describe. He'd discovered the Great Falls of the Missouri, a series of five linked waterfalls that would present a massive obstacle to the expedition. He sat down on the shore and feverishly wrote.

My ears were saluted with the agreeable sound of a fall of water and advancing a little further I saw the spray arise above the plain like a collumn of smoke which would frequently dispear again in an instant caused I presume by the wind which blew pretty hard from the S.W. I did not however loose my direction to this point which soon began to make a roaring too tremendious to be mistaken for any cause short of the great falls of the Missouri. . . . To gaze on this sublimely grand specticle . . . formes the grandest sight I ever beheld, . . . irregular and somewhat projecting rocks below receives the water in it's passage down and brakes it into a perfect white foam which assumes a thousand forms in a moment sometimes flying up in jets of sparkling foam to the hight of fifteen or twenty feet and are scarcely formed before large roling bodies of the same beaten and foaming water is thrown over and conceals them. . . . From the reflection of the sun on the sprey or mist which arrises from these falls there is a beatifull rainbow produced which adds not a little to the beauty of this majestically grand senery. After wrighting this imperfect discription I again viewed the falls and was so much disgusted with the imperfect idea which it conveyed of the scene that I determined to draw my pen across it and begin agin, but then reflected that I could not perhaps succeed better than pening the first impressions of the mind.

He thought about crossing out his words and beginning again. His imperfect description disgusted him. He left the account in his journal nonetheless, sensing that time dulls memory. In it, I read his rush of excitement, the thrill, and then his loss of faith in his ability to record it. You see him embark—then retreat into darkness.

* * *

Heading out, my lungs expanding, I think of the pig's lung I dissected in fifth grade; I stuck a plastic straw down the esophagus and blew into the straw. Careful, our teacher warned, don't inhale. The lung ballooned out. I think of the tests I took in the hospital with an asthma specialist. I blew into a tube that was connected to a computer screen. I was the wolf, and my exhales were meant to blow down the door of the pig's house. A scale at the bottom measured each puff.

Before I head out to run, I suck on the red plastic mouthpiece of my inhaler. My lungs expand. I bend to lace my shoes. There is the house, then everything beyond it.

Each foot claims a bit of earth. Sometimes when I leave I am reluctant. Sometimes I bolt into the dawn.

What I want more than distance now is speed. I want the sprint and thrust of a fast mile. The unbounded, reckless joy of that night in Maine when my body was both my body and something new that drove me with it. It is a statement against the body's frailty, written on earth by the body. The contractions astound me, the stop and go, the pull and release of ligaments and tendons, how the legs load and unload in one swing and the heel bears weight and then takes flight.

ELECTION DAY

The old beef farmer, whose cattle pick at the dry weeds in their pasture across our driveway, plowed up an acre of his land for me. I'm pleased to see it productive again. I watched him stop and throw bits of metal fencing and flotsam out of the disk harrow's path, leaning on the knee of his worn overalls. We are in a two-month drought. The creek where his cattle waded, where I looked for water moccasins, now weaves low and wretched through the crisp ragweed, gathering algae colonies in the deep cutbank eddies.

To the north, a forest fire is burning over hundreds of parched acres, and the smoke falls into this bowl of a valley, choking my throat, turning the sunsets sickly pink. People stop and take pictures of the light in the sky. I wake and burn brush in the newly plowed field. The soil is dust already. It seems like the right way to start, claiming gardens from the wilderness of neglect.

Our puppy has learned his name. He comes running to me through the billows of black grass-fire smoke. I read that the Druids lit bonfires on Samhain and passed the young cattle and sheep between the smoking pyres to cleanse them. It is that season. The dead walk briefly in the living world. But the Romans recorded the Druid's rituals, and history, I remind myself, is written by victors.

After I burn, I rake the ashes over the earth. I sow rye from my palm like the ancients. I can't bear the thought of the drive to Walmart where I could buy a grass seeder and finish this job by noon. Instead, I sweep my hand back and forth, blessing, blessing.

A great black murmuration of starlings shift and sweep like scattered equations or curses in the smoke. They don't land on my field, instead, they scratch at the dry pasture where the cattle haven't bothered to forage for weeks, or they crowd the skirts of the persimmon trees where the opaled fruit has grown sweet with rot. The first frost blackens the sweet potato vines, but I dug them already; one was shaped like a lightning bolt, charging straight into the red earth.

Then suddenly, with no warning from the forecast, Sunday dawns gray and damp. A steady cold rain quiets the dust. The starlings keep still to their roost. At night the clouds slip away, and waves of smoke sweep back into the basin. A super moon, closer to earth than any in decades, rises over the pasture, over the low smoke, thick as gunpowder. A witching hour. At dawn, I wait for the frost to leave the shadows. Holding a translucent rye seed to the light, I see the tail of germination fattening the husk.

LIVE FIND

On an unusually warm Sunday morning in January, I walk out into the woods. Sundays mornings are quiet, hauntingly so. In our little valley there is no sound from traffic, just red-tailed hawks screeching and bluebirds chirping in the dull vegetation. I had hoped, when I realized the silence meant our neighbors were attending church services, that I might hear hymns ring out between these hills. There are so many churches that it seemed plausible. I can hear the mechanic pounding with his air hammer, why not a gospel choir? Five churches line the four-mile road to town. Their names read like song fragments: First Baptist, Old-Fashioned Baptist, New Baptist, Good Shepherd Baptist, Travelers Rest Baptist. Their density suggests a mighty need.

While everyone else is looking to be found I am trying to get lost. I am tasked with hiding and then being found by our six-month-old German shepherd dog. My role in this "runaway" is that of the "live subject." The puppy is as new to this as I am. He's learning to find people, and I, a chronic mapmaker who obsesses over word choice and specifics, am learning to lose myself again, a skill that came to me naturally as a young girl. Logan has been bred for this role. His sire, Jackson, has been working as a search and rescue dog for five years and has found eleven subjects during eighty search efforts. His dam, Ellie, was imported from Slovakia and has been used as a cadaver dog since 2014. My boyfriend, Daniel, is the dog trainer, and it is he who holds a bottle of neon tinted powder above his head and puffs an ounce of it into the wind to determine its direction this morning. The powder drifts gracefully to the west.

I have no stamina for obedience training. My dog, Rosalita, a black-lab mutt who has no skill other than secretly cleaning the dishes in the sink, is evidence of this. I am Logan's human during the day while Daniel works at the hospital. It is easy to say I mother him. While I don't dress up the dogs, or carry them in handbags, I care for them in a way that is unmistakably maternal. During the first month we had Logan, I cut down my hours at work to spend long days with the puppy, watching him roll in the falling leaves, snooze, and chase cabbage moths. I told myself it wouldn't last, and a sense of present nostalgia tinted that whole season with gold, although the light that month was strange and metallic anyway due to the long burning north of us. The smoke drifted down and settled over the bowl of the plain, giving every photograph I took an unintentional filter. Sunsets were pink. Sunrises peach. That first month, Logan learned to ask to go outside, to sit and stay, to take himself into his kennel to sleep, and I learned to watch, to reward rather than punish, and that some moments are okay to slow down for. Chronic futurist, planning days and months and years ahead, I learned to settle, to note, as I had as a girl, the important routines of insects and birds, the path of the sun, the sound the wind made in each type of oak tree. Now Logan is thirty pounds heavier and full of bombast and inborn confidence that's explosive and startling in its focus.

When Logan sees Daniel reach for the bottle of tinted powder he knows what's going on. His eyes change, the pupils grow huge and dark as his brain fills with adrenaline. His long tail straightens. He leaps and whimpers and begs to go out with us into the yard, motivated to work more than anything else. Daniel has been training Logan to build a drive for this job that overrides anything primal: food, giving chase to deer, fear of darkness or new places, even the desire to play with toys. Watching the puppy quiver with anticipation, it's easy to imagine him bursting into caves or scaling the rubble of a bombed building, flooded with the motivation to search.

Daniel charts me a path down the driveway and up into the woods. Like the puppy, he is flushed with focus in these moments, and his dark eyes become warm with passion. Search and rescue is a volunteer effort, so when he pulls himself out of bed, after a long shift at the hospital because a hiker is missing off a trail, he won't get paid for the fifteen miles he hikes in the dark and heavy fog, nor for the hour he spends typing up a report. He paid to outfit his truck and for his own headlight, backpack, GPS tracking systems, boots and compasses, maps and first aid kits, not to mention the two German shepherds, Jackson and Logan, each of whom cost over $3,000. His reward is hearing that hiker, a sixty-year-old woman, call to him from the dark. After Daniel walked her out, back to the parking lot at the trail head lit with the spinning red lights from the fire department and the flashing blue of police cruisers, the woman turned and bowed to him, embarrassed, thankful but without words. I wonder sometimes how she will remember him, how she saw him that night, first on the trail, and then, in the strobing light of the lot. What does a savior look like? First, I suppose, it looks like a German shepherd, bombarding through the darkness.

I can hear Logan barking inside the house as I walk down the driveway; I'm not even lost yet, and he's ready to find me. I turn back and see Daniel on the hill, near the carport, his face raised to the wind like a raptor. He reads the wind for scent; as a farmer and gardener, I've learned to read it for weather. It is our shared language. I sit with my poetry books and he with his medical texts, but in the open air we read high and low pressure, dew point and jet stream. Today the wind comes up the throat of this small valley. This isn't my landscape, but I am learning it. We're transplants here. Through the summer I've worked my garden and found the soil shockingly red, stained like blood. I've researched the names of the insects; the huge wasps that pound on the screen at night are European hornets, and they live in a massive hive under the bridge of our driveway. Peaceful vegetarians, they are driven mad by lights in the night. Leaf legged beetles devour my tomato plants. Red, black, white, and green aphids cluster under the leaves of my collard plants. This is my form of searching, cutting down the background noise through specifics—catbird, cottonmouth, magnolia.

Scenting is about focus, about locating one thing in the mess of the world. Logan has the ability to do this naturally; he inherited it from his sire. Daniel decided to breed Jackson after he made a remarkable find in the fall of 2015. Jackson was searching for a teenage boy with autism who'd gone missing in the cold woods, a boy who was known to wander and hide. The dog was searching with another handler since Daniel was at the hospital. They swept along the bank of a lake, when suddenly the dog turned and jumped into the water. He swam five hundred feet out to an island. His handler squinted to see him burst through the low growth and up into the tree line of the island, but just as soon as the dog vanished, he reappeared and swam back to shore. Shaking off the freezing water he indicated that he'd found his subject. This indication looks different for every dog, but for Jackson, the signal is jumping up on his handler's chest. None of the search resources had mentioned that the boy might have access to a boat, so his handler hesitated. As if to prove his point, Jackson rushed back into the water, swam to the island, dashed into the bushes, and then returned to his handler. Officers located a canoe and paddled out to the island, where they found the boy huddled in a little fort made of twigs. Online news sources carried the story of Jackson's find. He was described as a "wonder dog," a K9 hero. Daniel received pleas through Facebook messages from people who managed to track him down, begging Jackson to come and look for their missing children. One woman wrote, "I Googled *best search dog in the country,* and Jackson came up."

Jackson works by scent, smelling humans on the wind. He's been trained to loop and search a landscape, listening, looking, tracking back and forth, covering ten miles while his handler walks just one. Dogs have an average of 220 million olfactory receptors in their noses. Jackson and Logan probably have more than that, while I, as I pick up the smell of fast-food fried chicken from a discarded Bojangles box on the roadside and the warm scent of oak leaves crisping in the sun, have just 5 million, making me more than a thousand times more numb to the world. It's hard for experts to pinpoint exactly what it is that dogs are smelling when they locate humans. Perhaps it is the little flecks of dust we scatter as we move through the world, scraps of hair and flesh. One handler we know thinks they can smell DNA. Dogs have located bodies under forty feet of rubble and identified human fingerprints that are over a week old. I've wondered what stories Jackson and Logan can smell when they joyfully stick their noses out of the car window and inhale information at fifty miles per hour. I envy them, breathing in knowledge while I am stuck identifying plants and bugs and learning the history of a place one small fact at a time.

I know that if I walk straight up into the woods from the road, I won't run into any houses. This tract of wood sits wedged between housing developments. From the stumps, soft with green moss, and the straight monospecies growth of Georgia pine, I know this forest was logged roughly thirty years ago. There are old roads sunk low in the land from long before that. Someone has cut four-wheeler trails through the pines and someone else, maybe the same person, has scattered corn and apples to bait deer and turkey. I've found their red shotgun shell casings and discarded soda bottles, but it isn't hunting season, so I don't walk in fear as I push through the brush along the roadside.

The woods are thick and prickly. If I wanted to run, I wouldn't get far. Holly bushes have sharp painful leaves. Blackberry choke the sunny spots. Climbing thorns loop up into the trees. Kudzu strangles. Mountain laurel grows dense along slopes and in the wet places near streambeds. I walk slowly to avoid being hurt by this place. When the vegetation grows in the summer, we won't be able to play hide-and-seek like this. It'll be too dense with the snakes out warming themselves and fire ants mounding.

Living with Daniel and the dogs, I am aware of how many people are missing. At any given moment, over ten thousand people are missing in the United States; some of them are runaways who wish to simply ghost out of their lives, while others need to be found. Being lost is a profound statement, a binary existence. It implies a negative, the B side of some bigger unit. Being found is an inclusive action. Often those who go missing are outside lines already—the young, the old, the sick, the suicidal, drug addicts, thrill-seeking hikers taking a stab at a knife-edge rim in the dark of a winter's night; each of these types of lost people behaves differently, and Daniel has trained the dogs to search for them all.

Those who seek to kill themselves with pills often head to high places where they can enjoy a spectacular view while they fade into death. Those with dementia wander but typically don't have the strength to take high or complicated paths. Those with autism tend to hide in confided areas like valleys or rock formations, or they are drawn to water. People who are blind drunk or high out of their minds move very quickly then stop and go no further. And of course, the dead move in their own ways, tumbling off ridgelines or washing downstream, caught in deadwood, or getting broken into smaller pieces by animals. This landscape conceals its dead easily, snake and swamp, thick brush, old mills, chain linked and haunted. Daniel's search team gets called more to recover corpses than to save the missing.

The dead are everywhere, I tell myself as I hike uphill. Bones in the ground like roots. History thick upon history, so tangled that only the dogs can pick out the important strands. My family's bones are back in Vermont, in a cemetery that looks into the folds of the Green Mountains. The woods there are more open, the white pine needles soft as makeup brushes on the cheek. I thought for a long time that those bones made that place my home until I found my heart was stronger than my skeleton and followed Daniel south. I've been walking for nearly fifteen minutes before I find a good spot to hide. There's a big old stump rotting on a rise that I can sit behind. If I were a lost person I might take shelter here, feeling safer for having something to my back. I sweep the holly leaves away, for they are as prickly as pins, and settle down to wait.

During early "runaways" when Logan was just learning to find me, Daniel would hold him, and I would jog just out of sight behind a tree or the edge of the garden shed. Gradually, I covered more ground, down into the pasture near the bank of the pond where our neighbor's cows retreated in the summer heat, or up onto the planting box of the grain drill under the shed roof where swallows darted and the last yellow jackets hummed. Then we started over again, but this time, the puppy didn't see me leave. I'd walk into the woods behind our house and lie down. When Daniel texted me I would yell out "I'm here," and using that single audio clue as an aid to the scent trail Logan would burst through the underbrush and leap into my lap. His reward, at first, was a jar of meat-flavored baby food that he'd lap from my hand. Slowly, Daniel replaced Logan's food reward with a toy reward, special rubber balls from Hungary that the puppy now prefers over Gerber's ham and gravy.

Logan is advanced enough now to no longer need an audio cue, so I won't have to yell "I'm here!" into the empty halls of Georgia pine, although there is something so definite and so desperate about that call that I almost miss it. I could open up Google Maps on my phone and see myself as a red pinpoint on the landscape, but the sentence, hollered at the top of my lungs into the woods, is so much more philosophical, so much more declarative than GPS or cell phone pings off the tower behind our house. "I'm here!" is a cry for help as much as it is a statement of existence. I don't really know where *here* is, maybe a ten-minute walk to the nearest house, a twenty-minute hike down to the state highway, but I can imagine getting lost in these woods of thick pine and low brush. There is just the slightest ripple to the earth, no jutting rock or grand slope, just a smooth wave like a quiet ocean.

I turn my cell phone to vibrate and settle into the silence of the lost person. I lie down and look up into the vanishing perspective of treetops. The wind, still blowing from the west, rocks them gently. I tuck my hands into my pockets—it's colder here on the forest floor in the shade of the old stump—and I can feel the chill of the January ground under me. The woods, which I thought before were quiet, start to rustle and crowd with noise. The trees groan and rub against each other. Something scratches in the underbrush.

Above me, turkey vultures spin in their updraft orbits, and I can almost hear their feathers rustling. They, too, are locaters of the missing, spinning like radar needles over the scent of death. I've read that they are an under-researched species, slighted by science, still cloaked in their hunched black wings, ugly angels of death. From a distance, though, they are geometric and soft. As a girl I used to try to see the landscape like the vultures did, from two hundred feet above. There was a grassy spot in our field where I would spend long summer afternoons of my childhood watching them glide through updrafts and trying to bend my mind into their little, sharp-beaked heads. I imagined my house with the garden and swing set, the field where I lay hidden watching the birds, then the woods stretching to the north, the river like a ribbon of light to the west, the state highway black and straight, the steeples of churches rising above the dense trees of high summer, the granite cliffs, the clock tower of Baker Library, the geometric grid of Dartmouth's green, the streets of downtown drawn like map lines, College and Main and Route 10. I loved maps, which seemed to start all my favorite fantasy books, and I taught myself to draw them as I explored the backyard, but all my maps started as the vision of birds spinning above the earth on the wind.

Lying in the pine woods, I feel again that same rush of adventure, a heightened sense of trespassing, I did as a child when I traipsed across our neighbor's property lines with my backpack full of comic books, a sketch pad and pencils, salami sandwiches, a stolen pocket knife, treats for my dog, and a bottle of water. What if someone found me lying out in the woods? What would they think of a woman who spends her Sunday mornings hiding behind a stump in leaf clutter staring up like a mystic at the hunting of vultures? Church must be out now because I can hear the crackle of rifle fire as kids shoot targets in their backyards, the roaring of dirt bike engines, someone's goat baying, a woman yelling, a weed whacker hissing to life.

I would have loved this task as a young girl, a serious child who valued both work and being outdoors. How many days did I spend lying in the woods, listening, I wonder, taking notes as if they added up to something. I grew up with no real religion and have been trying to hammer together a faith ever since. I steal Bibles from hotel rooms, I chant "Om" in the yoga studio, and I watch the morning sunrise through an amethyst crystal on my desk, which is supposed to encourage creativity. Paying attention to the world around me is the closest I've gotten to understanding what other people call God.

With Logan, Daniel would call my personal rituals "behavior patterns" and the type of work we are doing with runaways "patterning." Repeating something again and again until it becomes instinct, until it becomes a singular task that is more than the sum of its parts. The puppy is learning that scent and smell, run and jump, circling, and rushed locating are part a greater thing called finding. I am learning that paying attention is a type of salvation that starts with surrender. Lying down in the woods. Waiting to be found.

The wind makes strange sounds in the woods, sounds that I can't quite locate. Fear rises in me with the rush of trespassing, and now my senses are heightened. I can feel my pulse swell the veins in my neck. I focus on the treetops where they vanish into sky. I remember my best friend from elementary school, Katherine Blanchflower, who had a British accent and two passports that she showed me proudly, which conveyed upon her all the mystery and stories of the Old World. We took Sunday school together during the brief year that my family attended to such rituals. One Sunday, after church, we were playing together in a teepee we'd created by wrapping a Little Mermaid printed sheet around a cluster of deadfall pines that formed a triangular heap. The light through the sheet was bright, as through stained glass. Katherine whispered to me, and there was weight and sincerity in her whisper. "God," she said, "is just dog spelled backwards." I nodded like I understood, although I knew nothing of faith as a child. It wasn't until we got a dog that I learned to respect and care for something other than myself.

The first "book" I ever wrote was about my childhood dog, Velvet, so named because her ears were soft like the velvet dresses I imagined the Ingalls girls wearing to church in *Little House on the Prairie*. I saw in her something I wanted recorded, something notable and holy. I watched Velvet watching the world and followed her through the woods. We found coyote kills, bear dens, waterfalls, and abandoned cellar holes. I marked them all on my maps. In high school I wrote sonnets to her because she was all I knew of love, and when, finally, I dug her grave, I laid her to rest with pages of the comic book I had read with her all those summers in the woods. After her burial, my youngest sister told me that she'd never seen me cry before. I laughed, because I cry often, but always in hiding, and I remembered Katherine's wisdom, that semordnilap that switched the divine with a pet. Velvet was my translator; through her, I was able to learn the language of the world.

I am always more alive when I have a dog at my side. Shortly after Velvet's death, I purchased Rosalita, and I again felt that nerve open to the hidden secrets all around me. She dragged me out into the dark of nights as a puppy, and as she peed I'd see a full moon or the eyes of a moose tracking through the forest, high and beady. One January, I bundled up and took her out into a snowstorm, and then, suddenly, thunder shook the world and lightning shocked the whiteness, a meteorological wonder that I would have otherwise slept through. She found a beaver dam and a marsh dense with spring birds, and now when we walk along the back roads in South Carolina, she pulls me ahead, pointing out the junk but also the jewels of the day, a hiding infant fawn, a robin's egg shattered blue on the blacktop, a pine that plays another pine like a violin's bow humming strange and full of sorrow.

During November, when Logan was small, I walked the three dogs four or five times a day, on account of the puppy's tiny bladder, but also to introduce him to the world, to leaves, to water, to rock, to roadside, to mailbox, to grass, and to garden. All summer I'd avoided the dense woods, but as the leaves died and fell away, the forest seemed to open. Right behind our house I discovered two crumbling stone chimneys and an ancient electrical line running through the hearts of mature trees, a rusted carriage frame, a steam tractor's engine, a wellhouse, and a heart-shaped disk harrow buried in detritus. With the dogs, I saw the old roads' sunken lines, the cement bridge forms where once the brook had been forded, and closing my eyes, I knew this place better. I knew a bit of its history. Some nights, looking down into the lot with the two chimneys and the electrical line, I think I might see ghosts, but I never have. There are fingerprints in the chimney mortar though, much too old for even Logan or Jackson to identify.

I've been lying in the woods for twenty-five minutes and begin to feel that I might actually *be* lost. Maybe they aren't coming to look for me. I check my phone and then take a picture of my view up into the trees. Daniel and I are documenting Logan's training, Daniel with a video camera and me with my notes and letters. I can't help feeling that there is something special about the dog. He isn't a pet, Daniel reminds me, he is a tool, an instrument. He might save human lives one day. He will also be Daniel's partner, like Jackson is now.

Logan's existence seems to me something of a miracle. It took weeks of visits to Ellie and then to the vet to breed the two, Jackson being so well trained that he'd lost all interest in the business of sex. The last visit to the vet fell on the final day of Ellie's fertile cycle. When Daniel and I brought Jackson home, we stopped in the yard to watch a huge full moon rise over the pasture, strawberry red and shimmering in the humidity—marking the start of Logan's life.

After the puppies were born, we spent every weekend visiting with them. I set up a camera and recorded hours of footage as we played with them, ran after them, held each up to the lens. Daniel was looking critically for a certain set of characteristics, choosing the pick of the litter instead of a stud fee. By the time the puppies were six weeks old, we had narrowed the list from seven to two, a female and a male. For each dog, he wrote pros and cons, and then he ignored all that and went with his instinct, choosing the male puppy because he had never worked with a female dog before. Logan, stinking of his littermates, cried and scratched at my lap all the way home and only quieted when we opened the window and let the night air blow into the cabin. Searches are best conducted at night, when scent is easier to detect. Moisture rises. The wind settles a bit, and dogs don't get overheated. That night the full moon was marked with smoke. The Smokey Mountains were burning, Table Rock was burning, and all the smoke drifted down and turned the moon orange as a begonia.

Something crunches in the woods nearby. I shift and try to locate the sound. Two dark shapes move along the ground near me. My heart stops and then blood rushes into my face and neck. They aren't bear cubs, as my eyes had first read them, but instead huge wild turkeys, two toms out scratching corn at a feeding station. I watch them and see them spook— their tails fan out, then they tumble into flight, squawking up into a low roost on a pine branch. Something scared them.

I see Daniel first, wearing the red jacket he always puts on while searching. I know it smells like wild places and night air. He's scanning back and forth, looking for me. Then, low in the leaves, tumbling through draws and breaking up hanging vines, busting up the very fiber of the forest with his enthusiasm, I see Logan, running back and forth, chasing my skin particles, my fingerprint oil, my DNA. He's moving faster now because he can tell I'm close. A gust of air knocks the pines around and blows my scent right back into his big black nose, and his circles straighten into an arrow pointing right at my hiding place. He overshoots me first, then pivots and explodes into my lap, barely licking at the jar of baby food before he rushes back to Daniel. With all his strength he jumps and knocks his two front paws into Daniel's chest, indicating that he's made his find just like Jackson does, and then he sprints back to me.

I praise Logan, and Daniel tosses him his toy reward. I show Daniel the video I took on my phone of Logan bursting over the stump to find me, and he grins with pride. The puppy is still "on," in search mode, tearing through the woods, tossing his toy around playfully. Daniel reaches for my hand and leads me out the way I came, ducking under the vines and stepping over the thorn bushes. Logan circles us wildly. He looks like a little coyote, leggy and sharp in the ears.

Walking back through the pines, I rest my head on Daniel's shoulder, and we two-step around the thorns and vines. All around, the trees are talking, the mushrooms are sending out signals to each other through their underground networks, the animals are chattering, and kids are climbing into tree stands and forts.

The silence of Sunday is behind us now as we step out over the road and cross to our driveway, the puppy shepherding us home in sweeping circles. He is full of pride for having located me in all the mess of the world. Logan has a particular habit that Daniel says he's never seen in another dog. After he's found me, as we walk out, he circles back to check on me, as if he's concerned for me, that I might wander off again, that I might not make it. He runs up and bumps my hand with his nose. *Here,* he says, *you're still here. Come,* he says, *I know the way.* We hike up the driveway to our house where our two cars and our garden sit silhouetted against the crisp sky. I once was lost, but now I'm found.

ON TEACHING BRIAN DOYLE'S "LEAP" TO STUDENTS BORN AFTER 9/11

When I pick up the photocopies of Brian Doyle's short essay "Leap," my hands shake at its leanness, the bone structure of a ballerina, a body made for flying. Usually, the class reads pieces in rounds, one paragraph at a time, but because of its length and content, I've decided to read it alone, out loud. I take little breaths, sucking in the air, trying to settle the jumping choke in my throat.

"A couple leaped from the south tower, hand in hand."

I cry easily these days. My eyes slick over at every small moment of grace, a slip of elegant language, or the particular way a student reads out loud. I am teaching a nonfiction workshop for high school students in the very room where I took my first writing class fifteen years ago. The light in the space plays tricks on me; sometimes I'm sixteen again, stumbling through poems, my knee socks slipping, my uniform coming untucked as I slouch over the table. Or here, with a marker and a plan, at the head of the table. I'm so quick to tears at the sound of good writing that it doesn't seem remarkable to my students when my voice begins to break at the start of "Leap."

"They reached for each other and their hands met and they jumped."

My students cry all the time too. They come to class with eyes red from sleepless nights, from weeping. I remember this same feeling from the hunger of my youth, when the world is simply too large to understand, and you feel so small that nothing matters. Except, maybe, for what we work toward on the page. Every night at camp the bugle plays taps, laying the day in its grave. Then, in the private darkness after the last trembling note, when the loons start mourning for each other across the lake, as the girls shift and then fall silent in their bunks, I begin to cry. I cry because time seems to be overlapping, and I remember being a girl here. I cry because my students are so talented, so untamed, and I feel like an imposter trying to guide that energy on the page, a weatherman teaching a tornado. I cry because I believe in words, and sometimes in this world, art can seem tiny against impossible evils. When I wash my pillow in the laundry cabin, the fabric smells like salt and is printed with the wet lash strokes of wept-off mascara calligraphy.

"Jennifer Brickhouse saw them falling, hand in hand."

I notice at first that as I begin to read the essay, voice shaking, glasses glittering with tears, my students relax. Better to look away I suppose. Let off the hook, their minds wander, where, who knows—out the windows where the junior campers are playing frisbee on the great lawn, to the branches of the ancient oak I've told them was alive when Hemingway walked these Michigan woods, a fact that one boy from New York City has grabbed hold of. He wants, whenever we write outside, to sit under its wavering shade. They are thinking about the lunch menu, about the social at the girl's-side pavilion that night, about college, about their phones, which I've made them put away. But when my voice starts to stumble over the words, they stiffen. They look up. Two empathetic girls grow wet-eyed at my tears. The boy who loves the tree stares hard at the table's plastic gleam. It's not a long piece, so I trip forward until the room sits in breathless silence.

"But he reached for her hand and she reached for his hand and they leaped out the window holding hands."

The playwriting class next door erupts in laughter. The squirrels in the huge oak snap at each other and rush through the canopy like little storms.

I take my reading glasses off in a gesture that makes me feel assuredly like a writing teacher. I can feel the tears drying under my eyes.

The boy from New York is the first to speak, as he often is. "Was that about 9/11?" he asks, as if I have presented them with a riddle.

I swipe my hand across my wet cheeks. "It is," I say. I look down at my lesson plan, printed in the orderly manner of my morning brain, bullet-pointed, progressive, building to what I consider a fundamental revelation about the nature of nonfiction, that instead of being a selfish, self-centered, self-examining style, it is instead our best way to reach toward the universal. *Faith?*, I'd written in the margins, because this soaring sense of unity, this oneness, is how I imagine believing might feel. The lesson, as I've planned it, is about bringing in other voices, writing from the plural rather than the singular *I* that stands like the lonely ionic pillar of the genre. The *I* does not appear in "Leap" until several paragraphs into the essay, when Doyle finally enters the piece as the writer. But he isn't shaping the story or sharing his own. Instead, he's sharing his known language of mourning—prayer is failing him.

"I try to whisper prayers for the sudden dead and the harrowed families of the dead and the screaming souls of the murderers but I keep coming back to his hand and her hand nestled in each other with such extraordinary ordinary succinct ancient naked stunning perfect simple ferocious love."

I wanted to teach a lesson about collective memory, how a writer isn't just a singular voice. I'd planned on using a well-known event, like the terrible unfolding of 9/11, to anchor this in a writing prompt.

"We all have our stories about that day," I say, spreading my fingers over my lesson plan as if to steady myself. "I'm sure Doyle did too, where he was when he first saw the footage. Why do you think he chose not to focus on his story of an event that we all have personal memories of?" My students look confused. It had never occurred to me that they might not remember. In the voice of confession the class admits:

"I wasn't born yet."

"My parents told me how it felt in the city that day, it was scary."

"My dad worked in a building nearby I think."

"My mom was pregnant with me so I guess I was alive."

"I don't have a story."

But they do. We all do, even if the story is womb pink and fear hazed.

"Their hands reaching and joining are the most powerful prayer I can imagine, the most eloquent, the most graceful."

I was a high school sophomore in a class called Global Studies with much of my debate team, kids who wore power suits and dragged briefcases with wheels and dreamed only of attending Ivies like Dartmouth, whose campus engulfed our small town. We were starting the day, as we always did, by watching and then discussing the morning news, and so shortly after 8:45 a.m., we saw the first plane vanish into the North Tower. Then, eighteen minutes of frantic coverage later, with our teacher sitting with us, squeezed into one of those chairs with attached desks, the second plane sliced through the South Tower. I remember being too shocked to cry or think or say a single word. And then in a free period, shortly before school was canceled and we were bussed home, the towers collapsed in a cloud like a thunderhead, rolling across the face of the city. Facts flew around—Logan Airport. LAX. I knew my father was in the air, traveling from Boston to California on a business trip. He'd left that morning. I remember the silence in our living room as my mother and my three siblings and I waited for news, my mother holding the portable phone like an injured bird and then rushing to the kitchen, the receiver wet with tears, to hear my father's voice shouting "SAFE" over the chaos of the terminal. I remember my littlest sister's tears and snot on my skin. She's twenty-four, six years older than my students, and remembers nearly nothing of that day, just sitting on the couch when she should have been in school, and fear.

"The pink mist . . ." begins one of the emphatic girls, one of the girls who cries in the bathroom after the workshop, who cries on the beach at night when I'm sitting reading their essays, trying to listen to music on my earbuds so I can't hear them weeping, "it's . . ."

"See," says the quiet boy who prefers Nabokov above all the writers we read, "the jumpers." He holds up his phone, which he's been secretly using under the table. I had mistaken his posture for solemn introspection. The screen lights the photograph *Falling Man* by Richard Drew, which was printed in newspapers all over the country in the days following the attacks. A man plummets headfirst into death with controlled symmetry, but the image is just a frame, a slice of time that quiets chaos. The boy passes the phone around the workshop table, and I let them look. It's as if they need this confirmation. They need proof that this is indeed nonfiction.

I had intended this class session to be about unity and how a shared experience can sing on the page with the voice of a mighty chorus, but instead the class shifts toward investigation. The use of research and historical materials is a few days out in my syllabus, but here the students are thumbing through news articles on their phones, doing Google searches for photos published before they were born, before they were even pink flowers dividing in the womb.

"Can you remember when you knew history was being made?" I ask them, sitting now on the edge of the halo of tables, our tight workshop circle. My lesson plan tumbling away, I reach for clarity. "If not this moment, then something else. If not this memory, then another." The class thinks about this a moment, and I see their eyes scrolling backward. One girl's forehead is creased with wrinkles, and she's squinting her eyes as if to help her see better into a distant horizon.

"The election?" she offers.

"The tsunami?" her friend adds.

I grab a marker and make a list on the whiteboard. The students toss out memories until we've created a list of all the terrible moments in their lifetime. None of them are global, in the manner of 9/11 or the lunar landing, but then again their newsfeed is a continuous stream of tragedy, held in their small, open hands. Instead, what we generate are clusters of horror, natural disasters, police shootings, the sudden swift deaths of beloved musicians. What to do with this? I wonder at the litany we've intoned. I return to my tears.

"Jennifer Brickhouse saw them holding hands, and Stuart DeHann saw them holding hands, and I hold onto that."

The tears are not so much for the dead but rather about how we are all woven into these moments, all part of history even as history is being generated in the vast engines of time. Doyle's essay is about grief but also about rising. He's too skilled a writer, and too great a spirit, to work within only one emotion. The wail of grief gives way to this exclamation of joy:

"It is what makes me believe that we are not craven fools and charlatans to believe in God, to believe that human beings have greatness and holiness within them like seeds that open only under great fires, to believe that some unimaginable essence of who we are persists past the dissolution of what we were, to believe against such evil hourly evidence that love is why we are here."

I look at the list we've written on the board. The boy who is in love with the tree is gazing out at that old oak as if looking for guidance, and I was once him too, staring out that same window, at that same ancient tree trying to imagine the memories locked there in heartwood. My students have listed all of the terrible moments that united them through the gash of violence and fear, the gut-dropping whoop of horror, the shimmer in the glaze of an eye spilling into tears. What is it, if not unity, if not our desire to be more than the *I*, that allows us to imagine the space between a falling man and the street, or the way two hands lace quickly into a knotted embrace? The lesson is to write into that overlap, a leap out from the self into the beautiful mess of living.

LOVE LACE

There is a cube of double-reflection pyrite on my desk that, when placed over an image, reflects that image twice so that all the lines are doubled, hovering one above the other. You can't tell which is the ghost and which is the body.

The journal I wrote in all those months before was a cheerful lavender—I bought it in the basement of a bookstore at the university where you were once an undergraduate (sharp, dark as always, with other hopes and nightmares following you). Next to the bookstore—a memorial to the dead on the USS *Arizona*—two great chains are hung together under slowly dripping water that stains their copper permanently more ancient, blue as crystal. Still, I think of fists banging and steel so strong it boxed them in, only as it was meant to do, heavy and cool.

You ask me to stop reading the Bible—it'll do me no good—it won't mean to me what it does to you. I am too old now, too bitter. "Make your own gods," you say. I've always seen you as godlike yourself. You curse me to create the world alone.

All my thoughts lace me to you. I think not of a story or a word but of how to love you better, how to partner two wild things like hearts together.

Your friend tells me you complained to her of the white hairs growing beneath your dark curls. "I feel old," you'd said, but I love the hairs, their metallic shimmer like something a princess would spin for Rumpelstiltskin.

But age haunts us. A clock large with cleaver hands. Each year the eggs I was born with wash away in the tides. Broke, I learn that I am now too old even to think of selling them to some infertile belly. They are mine now only in their degrading, perfect state, and even though I know it's wrong, I imagine them as antique pearls, slightly yellowing with wear.

We try to dream the same dream. Jung (collective unconscious, blood in an alpine valley). Freud (white wolves in a tree). We drive to Savannah in a convertible, get all things cleaned, replace everything broken in our lives.

When we speak our conversations return to science (nature) and story (dream), woven together around a central point like lace. You like it best when I wear my hair in braids as I did often as a girl.

I say, "I will dream," and I do—but my dreams are forgotten, no use to any understanding, just flames in the night.

I envy the water in your shower, such immersion to cling to your every hair and lie shimmering in collarbone, ear scoop, fingernail crescent.

"You bruise easily," you say. I object. "How would you know?" I reply. "I've observed it," you say. You know the perfect point between the tongue and teeth to feel as if love has left a mark but has not, just a pulse, a memory of pressure, a salty caramel rock of heat.

We discuss elephant graveyards and early human burials over eggs at the Christian breakfast place, the girls—daughters, sisters, cousins—let us sit long after our plates are clean, the line of the hungry trailing out the door. In the moments of silence, they rush in with the bill. What interests me is the story—you, the science. We keep digging up the same bones of our separate truths again and again—they are everywhere—at breakfast, in our tears, in our idea of love.

Jung felt that the mandala was a universal human image, a mystic symbol deep in our shared space.

How many eggs do I have left? Pearls. Tapioca, bubble tea, slushing, dropping like pinballs down the dark chambers of my insides.

On the night you leave to clear your head, the sounds have never been so big. When you return, I don't let myself sleep for three hours until I'm confident that your resting body, wrapped in mine, will stay put until the dawn.

"I want to go to Mexico with you," you say. We are eating the street-style tacos, the one good dish at a local Mexican restaurant. You tell me about a peak you climbed over in Mexico City and the higher peak you looked upon. I remember a collection of cross-shaped necklaces hanging in your childhood closet, how you'd played them like strings, said they each had a story. If I could time travel, I would visit you as a boy, I'd watch like a hawk from some high point as you grew. I want to know the stories, but you don't pray anymore.

We wonder if Jung was crazy or just wanted a loosening—you say his drawings are childlike. I say they are methodical, nothing like the scrawls of a possessed artist.

More blood in my womb for a week. I sense something working there, hard, pulsing, and worry grows it until two tests prove that I am not pregnant, until a day passes and the stress leaches from me and I cut myself deeply shaving and bleed in the sheets and think *alright,* and then *no,* and my body is suddenly mine again, unchanged, a healthy, sour, decaying animal skin.

It doesn't really matter what you name the beast—it comes from that collective ancientness where a sound captures a single word—like *moaning,* like *no,* like *rot.*

In a dream I try to repeat often, you take our young son out on cross-country skis. I watch you with the dark rifles over your shoulders across the field outside our window and then you slip into the white woods. There's a fire and a baby in a cradle and outside my love is pinging off biathlon targets with a dark-eyed boy who looks like you and like me. In another dream we are both riding Indian ponies across the lip of a great cliff and a whole city has fallen into the ocean below. We have American flags wrapped around our shoulders like blankets. We look down into ruin and then wordlessly ride off.

The thing about depression is that it flattens the temporary into the always. Sometimes I half forget that things weren't always like this. You weren't always like this. In loving you today I hold on to what came before.

You are the only thing I pray about. I taught myself the practice of kneeling before my unknowing, my prayer of hope and asking for another. But it's selfish too, I know. Your light makes mine more so, your shadow my dusk time deeper.

I dreamed of a market in the rain. A girl who was my friend once was there with me. We both got our periods, heavy, and it was pouring rain. Her tattoos looked polished and bright.

We ran to our cars through a field of mud and farm trucks, red streaming down our legs.

A retired couple survived a fire by treading water all night in the center of their swimming pool while California burned down and over and through their home and garage and ate their two parked cars. Ducking the raining debris, their eyebrow hair singed, the water charred ashen. I want to write that scene. I want to know the color of their love when, at dawn, they walked out baptized into a world rethought, where trees are black and grass is white and mammals crawl back into the soft, sweet water.

Preservation is a forward-moving form of stasis.

A scientist on a podcast said of seeing a horseshoe crab shell for the first time as a girl that she wondered if there were ghost versions of herself in the world too, cast-offs that she'd left as she grew. The show was about crabs, not this idea, but I stopped there, derailed.

What dreams—the fan's cool sweeping on my cheekbones—your body curled behind mine like two cupped hands, we hold hands, we shift together, rolling in the dark sea of sheets—what dreams.

Dedication is a new word for love. Dedication is a formal basement, its gothic buttresses, a Roman arch supporting a thousand times its weight in flesh.

Jung dreamt of mandalas and of pine valleys full of blood, an old man speaking ancient tongues—last night I dreamt a future child, a son, woke you early to show you a book of baseball statistics. I also dreamt of tornadoes and fire knocking the world flat. We wandered back through the hallways of vast universities abandoned to the wind.

A MODEL HOME

I was once the kind of person who gave extravagant gifts. Each December I'm reminded of all the time I spent sewing bathrobes, hunting for signed first-hand editions, or piercing leather to craft slippers cuffed with coyote. I thought that these gifts said something about my love, that I tried so hard, and perhaps they did. I remember these gifts like I remember all things that I have crafted with my hands, with a kind of exacting, physical detail so precise that, given leather or flannel, I might recreate them again now, although the recipients are long gone from my life.

A gift, I realize, is intrinsically something you know won't return to you. A negative in the weight of our lives, transferred from one household to another. And so it shouldn't matter to me that I don't know where some of these objects ended up. They were given with no expectation that they should ever be mine again, even if I had labored over their making, buying, or hunting, as I did, searching for the perfect object that captured something other than the physical restraints of its existence, more than weight or texture, function or beauty. These weren't gifts so much as containers into which I poured all of my passion and confusion and hope. There is only one gift that I lost track of, one that disappeared before it could become beloved. I could show you the shape of the thing, but I couldn't tell you what became of it. Did we throw it away before our move off that bitter coast? Did we leave it behind in the cabin?

At the time of the gift's crafting, I was living on an island off the coast of Maine in a town that spent its summers dressed in the finery of waspy retreat, having replaced the Rockefellers with Martha Stewart, who was rumored to task her groundskeeper with sweeping clean the woods on her property each spring. There was lobster ice cream on the pier where the big cruise ships disembarked tourists for an afternoon and a National Park where Ansel Adams had captured the shell of a moonrise over birch swamps. A signpost showed where you could stand and shoot the same image, although it could never be the same. But come Labor Day the town boarded up—language which I always thought was purely metaphorical until I saw the plywood on the glass storefronts and the two-by-fours nailed across pub doors. They were closing for the season, the signs read, but also *to* the season, because in fall the winds rattled at those boards, clawing their way into every crack and mortar fracture.

The wind came into the bedroom in our cabin every night. One evening we watched as snow waltzed through the cracks in curls like you see in cartoons, circling white in the warm pine of the room. There were many other faults in the place, but we pretended to love them like we did most broken things because they had pasts, something that we, at eighteen, had very little of. All we had was a high school romance and a desire to become writers. Our parents encouraged this because they feared that if they weren't supportive, we'd simply vanish and become lost children rather than college freshmen at a tiny liberal arts college on an island in Maine.

The cabin was a kind of practice house, and as such, a perfect first home for me. I'd been making homes of the sort since I was a girl. To say that I played house as a child sounds gendered, and I just as often played a lumberjack or bushwhacking widow. The homes I built were mostly in the semi-wild wood lots behind the cul-de-sac where my parent's house rose up out of what had once been farmland but was now scrub pine and brambles with only the memory of the plow hidden in the old dumps I dug through as a child, uncovering the bones of bed frames and the friendly grills of ancient tractors. It was out in the mess of second growth, past where the tended lawn became field and the field became scrub, that I played home. I had homes in the trees—sometimes as simple as a board nailed high between two branches—and in the hollows where I fashioned rooms from the skirts of spruce branches, here the living room, here the kitchen, the bedroom, the hall. I'd lead my siblings and friends through these spaces, making sure that they saw what I saw in the dimensions. Later those same small hands helped me construct a treehouse, a huge teepee, an underground pit-fort dug into the soft loam of the field and covered with my favorite Little Mermaid bedsheet so the light came through all technicolor, and looking up I thought I'd made something like a cathedral for myself with nothing but a shovel and several long summer days.

Of course, I had a real home, but I spent a good part of my childhood running away from it. I ran away not for the usual reasons, or at least the reasons the children in my chapter books did—bad parents, dead parents, adventure—but with a plan to build a house for myself somewhere not too far down the road. I'd pack up my red flyer wagon with salami sandwiches, Kleenex for the constant drip of my allergic nose, and a neatly folded poster illustrating the history of the dinosaurs, which I considered my prized procession, this picture of the oh-so-obvious march of time. And off I'd go, up the gravel drive, along the dirt road of our neighborhood and out onto the paved shoulder of the fast state highway. I walked with a peaceful grin, the stupid joy of hope, knowing that the future was just a few more miles out ahead. In those days I loved the stories of children who lived alone in strange places like boxcars and the trunks of old trees. While I could only hear the train across the river at night, I did find a rotting oak in the backyard with a hollow so large that, for a while, I could squeeze inside and look up into its center. It wasn't big enough to build a fire in or to set up a bed, but for some time I was small enough to imagine it as a home.

An adult only needs so much space, a child even less. I was small as a girl and grew into a woman short enough to walk the deer paths in the forest without so much as a bend in my back. I liked as a girl, and still do, the feeling of being surrounded. I loved best the small places and the creatures that burrowed and nested in them, luxuriating over the soft grass beds of white-tailed deer and the little circular openings of the homes of mice in the hayfield. There was an exactness to the size of these homes and a practical grace to their architecture, surely more beautiful than the big boxiness and high ceilings of my family's home, where even with my door locked, I couldn't seem to find a second of peace. I took to hiding, building holes in my closet and under my desk where I could read, draw, and become the cartographer of new worlds for my characters and myself. I traced the maps of Middle Earth and sketched my backyard with the same deliberately archaic lines.

Eventually, I outgrew these places, like I did the playhouses and forts I constructed. One board remains in the crown of a knotted pine in my parents' front yard, and looking up I wonder at my bravery to climb so high just to gain the sort of aerial perspective that my mapmaking encouraged. I remember a moment of sharp sorrow as a girl when I outgrew a particular play structure in our basement. It was a bright plastic thing with walls that fit together like puzzle pieces, a short slide, a little platform, and a climbing ladder, but what I loved most of all were a series of large round holes, like Swiss cheese, passing through one wall. Because of these holes, I called the place my mouse house and played at squeezing through each hole, from top to bottom. At first it was easy, but then it became a game of contortion. Finally, one day in grade school, no matter how I angled or pushed myself, I could no longer fit through any of them. I was too big, having outgrown the house. I wept at the realization that the dimensions of my physical self no longer fit a space I called home.

Perhaps the whole process of growing up is more a process of outgrowing. I think of snakes and crustaceans building new homes around themselves. But maybe the metaphor is too physical. Homes are more than dimensions. You might call a lesser structure a house or a living space. Home has that big wide *o* in it, like *hope*, a noun that means more than it describes. A home, I knew even as a girl, said something about who a person was, what they wanted, what they had, and what kind of future they might be capable of creating. My family's house and the choices they made in it—my mother's music room sprawling over a third of the ground level, my father's meticulous study of the family's growth in yearly photo collages marching like the ages of the dinosaurs across the second-floor hallway. What they put in it altered the dimensions of the space, but the home itself wasn't unique. My best friend had the very same house.

Katherine's family lived in a similar neighborhood a few miles up the state highway. We took the bus to and from school together and would often pretend that we were orphaned sisters being sent off by train into new families who had adopted us separately. We'd cry as we parted, walking down the steps to our waiting mothers who, at least for a second, still looked to us like strangers. Katherine was just as good at playing make-believe as I was, which was probably why I liked her so much. For many years we slept in the same room in our matching houses, and when we grew older both of our families built rooms in their attics, except that my family created two rooms while hers kept the space an open loft, one so big and empty that when we stayed up there overnight, I lay awake long into the dark, spooked by the exposure.

I made other observations about the matching houses. Her parents didn't have a music room as we did. Instead, they had a playroom where we could watch cable TV. And years later, after her parents got divorced and mine stayed together, her father put a swimming pool in the backyard, and I remember soaking in the chlorine while he brought out sodas and set bowls of chips on the patio furniture. By that point, there wasn't too much alike between Katherine and me, besides our houses. Eventually I noticed only the differences and forgot that we walked the same floors and slept in the same room.

It was around this time that I began designing my dream home. There was a game the girls played called MASH RAP, the letters of which stood for future houses and financial standings—mansion, apartment, shack, house, rich, average, poor. Not included in the title but in the following components of the game were categories for husband, car, number of children, and job. The dimensions of life could be reduced and predicted just like that. You picked a number, and the number gave you all the answers. The goal, of course, was that it would create some sort of predicament where you were rich but lived in a shack and were married to the bald gym teacher, had fourteen kids, drove a Range Rover, and worked as a belly dancer. The only constants were those of home. In the Game of Life boardgame, I loved to sort through the house cards, weighing each potential self out, a woman who would fit into a split level, a woman in a Victorian estate, a cabin, a colonial.

One of the traps of aesthetics, and perhaps of creativity itself, is that it constructs the spiritual out of physical materials—a woman into a house, a dream into a space. And so the process of building homes was always about *being* and about *being known,* and the home itself was me and us and all of the things I hoped for.

I was once told by my allergist that dust is mostly human skin, and I've come to think of growing as casting off and

leaving behind small ghosts, so ordinary that only by accu-
mulation do they cause any notice. All the possible women
I've been in all the places I've called home, going on as if I
never left. A woman in Oregon, in Michigan, in California,
South Carolina, Maine. The dream women go on living in
their dream homes like the one I designed in fifth grade, which
contained on its first floor an enclosure for the Yellowstone
wolfpack whose restoration I had supported through allow-
ance-sized donations. Above the wolf pen there was a movie
theater, and on the roof an Olympic-sized swimming pool. If
growing up is the casting off of potential futures, the woman
who lives in this house is the one I hope to become again, our
forms aligning. She is nothing like the woman I was when I set
up home in the cabin.

The house in Maine was a practice house. Not just for me,
learning to live with another, to cook and clean and care, but
for the house itself, which was built by our landlords as a sort
of trial before they felt confident constructing the larger and
more complicated home in which they now lived, just a few
hundred feet from our southernmost eave. The practice house
had been a success, I suppose, in that it convinced them that
they could do better. But, as the landlady said when she took
us on our first tour, they had made mistakes. Nevertheless, we
paid her a deposit, coaching each other through the process of
writing a check for the first time.

It wasn't just tiny, it was miniaturized. Small houses have
their own expectations of space and dimensions, which differ
from that of their larger cousins so that a small house is not
simply a larger one shrunk down to scale. But the cabin was
clearly designed to be bigger, and its measurements had simply
been reduced in construction so that the ceilings felt too close,
the turn in the stairs too sharp, the shower head so low that
even I had to stoop under it. There was a porch, but it was
too shallow to put a chair on and the backdoor leaped out
into space with nothing beneath it. For all of its bad design,

despite all of the halfmoons of missed hammer marks in the soft pine boards, I loved it because it was a home.

That fall, as the boards nailed over the storefronts on Main Street and the winds came off the Atlantic, I began to wonder if I had made a mistake. I disliked the college and the coursework and spent most of my time working in a general store on the lower floor of a two-hundred-year-old house with a resident ghost, where a crowd of lobster fishermen streamed in each morning, flushed bright from the sharp wind. They bought coffee and breakfast sandwiches before dawn and beer and cigarettes at dusk, as regular as the tides. One of them proposed to me, getting down on his knee in front of the register, offering up a toy ring he'd pulled from a trap in the bay. I told him I was taken and flashed the gold band I wore on my left hand, a promise that never became any more than that, but for a season, held the weight and heat of something real. He asked me instead to come to a bonfire he was hosting on the beach. And later that evening, when the real darkness washed in, I left the cabin with some sort of excuse and drove around, coming so close to the fire on the coast that I almost wept before turning back to the pines and the practice house.

It was there I learned not to store flour next to laundry detergent, to keep Halloween candy away from mice, and that almost everything can grow stale. But I remained hopeful. At nineteen I suppose hope was my crucible. Still, there were moments when I would pause at the windows and see myself from outside and wonder what that girl was doing. This kind of splitting in my case is purely a creative projection, but I suspect that for many years the practice produced the same kind of psychic damage that near-death experiences or psychosis may have on the self—a doubling that only reinforced the complicated fractals of my dream homes and dream selves, looking in and looking out.

It's not the fault of the house that a person would live and dream such things within its walls. After all, homes are meant as containers, shaping the vast churn of infinity into something linear, a life, as we understand it, having a beginning, middle, and end, a story containing plot, rising action, climax, and falling action. Naturally, we play the heroes of these dramas so that a house is a story and not just a realization of walls and timber. But I'm still drawn to the exactness of the dreams that these spaces contained and to my ability, years later, to move within rooms that may now be cluttered, abandoned, or demolished.

That winter I built the cabin again and then, after gifting it away, it vanished. It was a scale-model architectural rendering constructed from cardboard and popsicle sticks, which I had crafted as part of my art class for pedagogical reasons that I comprehend now as little as I did at the time. Everyone at the school majored in human ecology and was required, as a freshman, to build such a thing. There was doubtless some sort of hippie philosophy behind the project, as there was behind everything at a school where we were tasked with miming the deforestation of New England as part of the freshman icebreaker. Although we could pick any structure we wanted, I constructed a model of the cabin in the pines. I charted the place with the cold metal tongue of a measuring tape, and night after night I stuck wood to cardboard until my fingers were strung with hot-glue spiderwebs and the cabin rose from its yard of plywood, perfect in its exactness. There the shallow porch, the cramped loft, the door to nowhere, the windows through which we looked in and out.

I gave this miniature house to my love for Christmas. I remember him startled at the thing and then peering inside, his eyes walking the floors we lived in during those days. He could hold it in both hands like a tray, and it weighed nearly nothing, just balsam and paper. His hands were soft, his fingers round, his skin fair. But I can't tell you about his wrists. I've forgotten the dimensions. I can't tell you what he said or where he set the model, and I can't remember what became of the thing when we moved a few weeks later, giving up on the dream of college on the coast of Maine and packing up for the Pacific.

I didn't think much about the place in Maine until years later when I drove by its twin. I stopped and pulled over on the shoulder of a quiet suburban street. There it was, the same dimensions, the same odd size of the practice house but in a new town, a new state. I learned later that the plans were sold as part of a prefabricated kit published in the seventies to include not only blueprints but also instructions so that anyone could follow along. The hopeful but unskilled builder can download similar plans now for tiny houses, container houses, hobbit houses, all kinds of hopeful, small places where given very little you can imagine yourself having it just right.

I lived in another duplicate house years later, a cottage on a creek in Vermont. It was so cold in that place that my cat jumped from chair to chair like a child playing don't touch the floor. A decade later I woke up in a house I had quickly toured before renting in a rush and realized that it was the same house as the one by the creek. Rising from bed, the dimensions tripped me up, and walking to the bathroom I was overcome with a feeling of full-body déjà vu until I realized that it was truly the same space, the same floors and rooms and proportions. Like the cottage in Vermont, it was built by a couple escaping the city and wanting to learn how to put together something real with their hands. I haven't been able to find the name of the kit or locate the exact plans. It's out there somewhere, a ghost of a house I've lived in twice.

The model house was gone by the time I lived in Oregon, but it's my apartment there in Portland that I haunt the most, although I never thought of that rainy city as home. Ever since I moved out, I've dreamt that I still rent the place and that it is sitting empty, looking over the Wilmette toward the peak of Mt. Hood, a container for a dream that died a long time ago. I wake, worried that the rent check hasn't cleared or that the maintenance department needs to install a new fridge and wants a key that I haven't held in over a decade, a key I remember slipping into the mail slot of the manager's office on a bright morning with my car loaded for a cross-country trip back to the East Coast. When I returned to the city years later, I drove by the place and saw beach towels hung to dry on the railing and felt myself split again—worried about the towels blowing off the third-floor balcony, even though they were not my towels and I no longer lived there.

Perhaps I fixate on space because I've spent much of my time farming, measuring out the earth with my body, my almost exactly five feet of body. Or maybe it's the running, training for long races that teach the body and the mind to mark out miles against the roll of the road. Whatever the reason, I find myself creating identity through dimensions. Since the model house, I've had the chance to design a life-size space for myself and see it rise out of raw materials, from open air to a container for a future I hope grows toward the light. But I can't stop thinking about the ghosts that move through the houses in which I once lived, sometimes briefly, sometimes for many seasons. I wonder at the girl who made that miniature house, what she hoped it contained as she gifted it. How extravagant an idea to craft a model of something that was still living, still forming in the unraveling of the everyday, a place where she washed dishes, made pancakes from her father's recipe, grew tired of some poets and fell in love with others, and learned many things: how to bundle beneath snow devils to stay warm, how to keep a house open to the heat and closed to the cold, how to kill a trap-caught mouse with a frying pan, how to write a check—signing her name in her school-girl's cursive—and how even in a dream house dreams can be outgrown.

INK

It begins to rain coldly, wind blowing, as I walk the city, so I wait out the weather in the Settlement Exhibition at the Reykjavik City Museum. Elevated above the ground, as if upon a funeral pyre, the shape of a Viking longhouse has been reproduced with entryway, sleeping quarters, and cook fire. Along the walls are scraps of bone and driftwood where letters, maybe symbols, have been scratched out. Notes of possession, the museum explains. In the children's area, a pile of bones and a mystery for little ones to solve. At the threshold of the longhouse, buried among the wall's stones, the skeleton of a woman, three cats, and the skull of a horse were discovered. *Who*, the display asks, *do you think she was?* Outside it is still raining, so up the street I slip into the Tattoo Expo held in the ballroom of a hotel where crystal chandeliers shatter down the fancy wallpaper. Mostly the kids here are getting flash pieces inked—pre-drawn and standardized, the easy choice. Smell of wet cigarettes, nervous sweat. I strip off my jacket and roll up my sleeves—the only time my arms are exposed on this cold island—and an artist from Austin, Texas, looks at my skin and its art and tries to get me to pay for a quick bite of his needle. *No.* What would it mean? A tattoo is like a language and something that outlives the spirit. Languages die or live or survive like people, through love. Sometimes no one remembers them anymore, but our human eyes recognize the scratch as something more than the fissures of time or the shaving of a glacier.

ON NIGHT

Night* is an absence, a void. The sky is no longer awash with blue or turbulent with great clouds. All of that is erased. Our eyesight, one of our species' greatest gifts, is rather useless in the pale. To those of you in cities and the vast suburban warrens, I realize that your night is not the night that I am speaking of here. I am speaking of rural night, night in the country. Night without streetlamps, without spotlights, without light pollution, without control. We gave up things as we moved down out of the trees, exchanging the nocturnal vision of arboreal apes for the somewhat less light-sensitive sight of the biped. Now, with two feet on the ground, we can't see much in the night. It's only in the full-moon's brilliance that we might still walk the forest without tripping over our hiking boots or take the dog down the road and still see her black shape at the end of the leash.

It was on these nights that our species first watched wolves hunt in packs and learned from their organized pursuits. But it was also on these nights that we were hunted. The full moon represents a sort of equilibrium between prey and predator. For the most part, prey species (deer, zebra, sometimes us) do

---

* Know that when I say *night,* I mean the time between sunset and sunrise, and when I say *darkness,* I mean the absence of light. Language is sometimes too full of metaphors to be exacting, and what I'm trying to describe doesn't seem to have the proper words, so any other term that I use has been chosen very carefully.

not see well in the dark, while predators (wolf, tiger, house-cat) are gifted with varying forms of night vision. The earth is given over to the hunter at night. Artemis strings her bow and Freya harnesses her giant cats to hunt in the full moonlight. Those who do not hunt hunker. Bed down. Take to dens and nests. The solitary join the herd, for there is strength in numbers. Perhaps the full moon haunts us because we can see death coming. It is both the easiest sliver of the lunar cycle to hunt in and the most challenging because the prey can see you coming. We think of all beasts as taking to the night, and perhaps for those who live in the semi-permanent half-light of cities and suburbs, this is now the case. But out past the reach of streetlights, many species are crepuscular, moving about at dawn or dusk. It is at this time that I can hear the woods around me walking.

There is a well-worn path through the snow about five feet into the trees that loops around my yard with careful consideration of the line between human space and wildness. Occasionally a bold individual will strike out into the garden or take advantage of the driveway's plowed avenue, but for the most part, the night creatures keep their distance. It's not them that I fear. Nor is it the darkness. I am happy to go out onto the logging roads with my headlamp. What I know about the night comes to me in my bed, creeping inside and sitting heavy on my chest.

When I was a girl, the doctor said I had night terrors. For nearly a year I couldn't sleep on my own. The terror at night was unlike any kind of fear I knew during the day. I can't remember being shy or afraid to speak my mind. As a girl, my hand was quick to shoot up in class. I climbed the tallest trees in the forest, trees that make me dizzy now with the danger. My night terrors were not a bad dream but an overall, full-body feeling of horror. I'd wake sticky with sweat, the sheets pressed to me. My heart would be racing. It was so bad that I grew afraid of sleep, afraid to close my eyes. None of the sheep counting or books read out loud worked for me. I clung to wakefulness, fighting against sleep. During these nights I lay on a camping mat in my parents' room and watched the red eye of the smoke alarm blink, the digital numbers on the bedside clock shift, my parents' forms toss under their covers, the stars spin outside.

The one dream I remember from those terrors was much like those nights alone, awake. In the dream a fire would move through my family's house, turning them all to ash in their beds. I alone would be spared, and waking in my dream I'd go to each pile where my father, sister, or brother had been. I'd rush to call 911, but the phone was a puddle of plastic. And so, I'd go sit on the smoking front step and watch dawn through the big white pine in the middle of our yard, waiting for whoever or whatever was coming.

I had this dream so many times that I could feel it coming—there was a certain weight to it on my chest. Those who suffer seizures often report a smell that precedes the attack, almonds, cleaning products. An ex-boyfriend smelled burning toast. At night I just felt pressure and a kind of helplessness, like a weighted trap sinking beneath the waves. What I know about night starts here.

The terrors went away, but I have never been able to sleep easily. For many years I feared the falling, the pressure, the ache of being awake when everyone else was asleep. After all the other girls had curled into their sleeping bags and the room was quiet, I would lie awake at sleepover parties and feel so alone that my heart would break. I'd look at them, their faces, their restfulness, and know that I wasn't like them. There's a divide between those who can sleep well and those who can't. It's a skipped beat in the deep rhyme that marks out our days. Night is that divide. Oh, I'd look at those girls with envy. The sleepers. The peaceful ones.

Let me make this clear though before I continue. I want to sleep. I am good for nothing when the sun goes down. I am not the insomniac pacing or the workaholic burning the midnight oil in front of oh-so-many screens. In fact, for all of my years of education, all my varied terms of employment, I have never once pulled an all-nighter. I've worked late, yes, but never until dawn. Late for me is the turn into the new day, and my phone is reliably set to an embarrassingly early bedtime. I work best in the morning and have learned to plan my day around this circadian cycle. I joke that it was my many years of farming or the early classes I taught in the gym, but I've always been this way. Eager for the night to end.

My sleep is perhaps best described by those who have endured a night with me, some of whom were probably too polite to say anything. Those who have spent years by my side are better informants, reporting on my behavior from the other side of waking. Even my sisters will tell you of how I haunted our shared bedrooms, shaking the bunk bed, startling them awake. The sleeping me isn't some kind of alter ego. In the night I do exactly what I do in the day. I'm sure someone is searching the web for a diagnosis, and from my own research, primarily from the works of the blessed Oliver Sacks, I believe I have some form of sleep paralysis. There. Stop worrying about terminology. I'm not a doctor, although I sleep with one, which may give some credit to his careful but often startled observations.

EXAMPLE 1:

The doctor and I were vacationing in Italy. Our Airbnb was across from the Colosseum and afforded startling views over the ancient city. It was nearly perfect, except that at night a flock of what seemed to be a thousand birds roosted in the one lonely tree outside the window. Roosting is probably the wrong term—they partied. At some point during the night, I sat up in bed and told the doctor to listen, that the kids on the street below were talking about how loud the birds were.

He told me he didn't think so. They were drunk and ranting in Italian, which neither of us fully understands. I said, "Yes, yes they are." I heard the word for bird, and then, pulling a pillow over my head, I went silent. In the morning I woke remembering a dream in which people were talking about the birds. Over espresso, at the café downstairs, the doctor told me that I hadn't been dreaming. I had been in bed saying those very words. I sulked in my embarrassment all morning, stumbling over the cobblestones, trying to remember the feeling of wakefulness in the night.

EXAMPLE 2:

When I was a CrossFit coach, I worked at a gym that had two options for completing the four-hundred-meter run. Some people preferred the down and back on the rail trail while others liked to circle around the building and parking lot. Depending on the season and the traffic, I'd instruct the class to run one route or the other. Sometimes I'd let the class decide, so they'd all take off, some out the front door, some out the back. One night during this time, I nudged the doctor in bed and, shaking him awake, asked him which way he was going to run. He responded, terrified, by asking me again and again if I was asleep. I insisted that I wasn't and needed to know which route he'd take. "Please tell me you are asleep!" he yelled, and I startled up a layer of consciousness into the bed, and there I was, sitting, pointing, and I muttered something and slunk away, hiding under the covers.

EXAMPLE 3:

I was a farmer at this point in my life, and I loved my job and the land more than anything. One night I woke knowing that the temperatures were going to drop and that the cucumbers, freshly transplanted in the summer fields, needed to be covered with a protective fabric. I rushed out to them, and then something flashing and yellow caught my eye. I blinked awake. It was the middle of winter, and I was in my cabin, five miles away from the farm, and the town plow was rounding the stonewall on the corner, lights flashing in the falling snow. I remember the way the two realities pulled at each other, the one in which it was a cool summer evening and the one where I stood with my feet on the cabin's tiles, watching snow stack up against the windowpane. The competing visions fought for a while until I realized there was nothing to do and went back upstairs to bed, still deeply worried about the cucumbers.

So, you can see from these examples that the woman I am in the night is very much the woman I am in the day. Exactly the same, in fact. Giving the same speeches and asking the boring everyday questions that populate my life. The night woman is bossy, talks a lot, and eavesdrops, all traits that I possess when the sun is up. What I fear about the night is that I have no control over this other woman. I put myself to bed, and she rises. She goes on doing my job while I sleep. I wake feeling worn out, and two, three cups of tea or coffee later, I still feel thin. Not fully present. *Like butter scraped over too much bread,* as Bilbo says to Gandalf. One person stretched between two realms.

What I know about the night is gathered from these kinds of stories, from the terrors of my childhood and from the few times in which I've outlasted the dark and stayed awake from the set of the sun to its rise in the eastern sky. Not all-nighters in the sense that my students think of the term but attempts to see the night through to the end, like an explorer crossing through uncharted territory. I suppose it's rare to have only two such tales to tell. But for me, there is little to say about that void except that the world continues without me, which is perhaps as sad and as real as watching the sleepers in their peace.

The first night was spent down by the river at the farm. We had a fire by the bank that lasted long into the night, until it was just my two good friends and me. Everyone else had crashed in tents or pickup trucks, but we remained around the coals, drinking, smoking, staring at what felt like the same space in the twisting smoke. The farm then was a place that I knew like my own body, a second skin, and all around me it was pulsing with July insects, growing, stretching toward the zenith of the summer. I could hear where the fields ended and the hedgerow rose, could smell the fog settling on the cool back of the current. "What is that?" my friend asked. "Birds," my other friend said. I looked up. The sky was the palest shade of pewter. "The sun's coming up," I said, and we smiled at each other as if we had survived something and come out on the other side. That communion was so different than my typical solitary night.

And in fact, when I stayed awake again until dawn, I was with another group, captaining a twenty-four-hour relay trail race. I stood at the central pavilion with my timetables, sending off runner after runner and waiting for them to return up the hill, their headlights swaying. I watched the moon rise full through the pines and stumbled out at 4:00 a.m. onto the trail for my leg of the relay, a rough 5K up a washed-out creek bed. There was fog along the water and the headlamp choked the view, so I ran for a while in the darkness. When I got back to the pavilion, some of the sleeping runners were up, wrapped in blankets, the fires had died down, and light was cracking open the edge of the tree line.

Later, I wanted to write about night within the lines of the relay-race story, anchored in the scene, talking about darkness, but research and memory keep shifting, growing outside the limits of the essay. In the margins of notebooks, I draw constellations of ideas, connecting each with a single thin line from my pen. For instance, how I can connect terror to my waking world, rest to fear. The sky to my father. How once we lay in the snow when I was a girl and watched the ordinary space above our house melt with flowing energy, the northern lights shimmering. Then I draw a line to the myths we read together, gazing through the eye of a telescope as my father illuminated the heavens with the shapes of sisters, hunters, swans, and faithful dogs. *Some of the stars you see are already dead,* he told me. *We are so far away that their last light is still catching up to us.* What a terrible thought. Like letters opened too late. *The sky is full of the dead?* Forever after I've looked up in fear, imagining the cold eyes of burnt-out stars. They watch me through the windows, and I have to pull the shades down tight.

Draw a line to death. Draw a line to the darkest fears that rise at dusk. To the nightmares galloping into sleep. The nightmare herself riding upon your chest, Goya's bats clattering in the shadows. *And that,* my father said, pointing to the flash of a satellite, *is man-made,*** *circling the earth.* I circle the word *circling.* And then draw another line to orbit it. Space is full of pollution and trash, bits of rockets. I spin out into it. Past the memory of my father, past the line of the story I'm

---

** In 1977 NASA shot the *Voyager* spacecraft into the vast darkness of the night sky. Each of the two space probes contains an audio record, a sort of letter in a bottle to be read (in this case listened to) by whatever intelligent life the craft reaches, a time capsule stuffed with an introduction to Earth. The music producer Jimmy Iovine split his time between the Voyager project and the sound rooms at Atlantic Studios, where he was working with Bruce Springsteen on the album that would become *Darkness on the Edge of Town.* He had a love song already on the album, so Springsteen gave a half-written demo to his friend Patti Smith, a single-track cassette tape on which he'd scribbled "Because the Night." Smith let the cassette sit around her apartment until one night, after a long-distance phone call with her boyfriend, she popped in the tape and started writing. "Because the night belongs to lovers / Because the night belongs to lust / Because the night belongs to lovers / Because the night belongs to us," Smith sang.

trying to chase out on the page. It's so easy to drift from one point to another when writing about the night. It gets slippery, and I feel myself splitting as I did by the window or in the bed, speaking while dreaming, dreaming while waking, neither here nor there, just circling. But in my dreams, I still wake alone and go out to sit on the front step. The sun is rising in the east, and I'm waiting for something to come down the gravel drive. Behind me, there are only ashes.

MUSE

On a rainy Sunday deep in January, Daniel and I walk to the Greenville Museum of Art to view an Andrew Wyeth exhibit. Rain muddies the gardens and floods over the sidewalks. We zip our coats up to our throats and hunch our shoulders as if they can shelter us. The rain isn't too cold; already spring is breathing green in the mountains. Inside the lobby an elderly volunteer takes our dripping jackets and hangs them on a gold metal rack. There is no entry fee. Everything downtown is still clean from its upgrade. There's a shine on everything here.

Daniel finds my hand. I am already homesick at the thought of Wyeth. His dark New England landscapes are poetic maps for me. I have walked them often—the cornfields of November, the spring orchards, the winter beaches—and felt their bite, their saltiness. They aren't real of course; Wyeth was a romantic. Although many call him a realist because he painted each blade of grass, or strand of hair on a woman's head, his paintings are fairytale twists. Think of Christina World, the woman crawling over a tall wave of grass to a gothic farmhouse, her pink dress worn, and know that Christina suffered from Charcot-Marie-Tooth disease, a form of genetic polyneuropathy that robbed her of the ability to walk. Her hands curled up like buds. She crawled through her world. But the model was Wyeth's wife, Betsy, turned away from the painter with the wind taking her dark hair out of its pleat. Wyeth layered things like this, making someone something else.

He'd been trained in storytelling. I explain this to Daniel as we walk on the shiny granite tiles. Andrew's father, the renowned illustrator and painter, N. C. Wyeth, taught all five of his children to paint in their private country house in Chadds Ford, Pennsylvania. There were busts of Beethoven and Lincoln to sketch and volumes of Tolstoy, Emerson, and Thoreau to memorize. While N. C. Wyeth illustrated *Treasure Island*, *Robinson Crusoe*, *The Last of the Mohicans,* and *Rip Van Winkle,* Andrew explored the New England landscape, living, as he said, like Robin Hood. By the time he was a teenager his father took him to his formal studio, where Andrew received the only formal art lessons he would ever have. When he was twenty, his first art show sold out. A few years later his father died suddenly when a train struck his car. For the rest of his life, Andrew would paint the landscape around the tracks where his father died.

His paintings darken the white walls. I see her first, and then I feel Daniel drawing me forward. We stop ten feet away from the big tempera painting. Even from this distance I can make out every eyelash and laugh line.

"Is that his wife?" Daniel asks.

"No," I explain. "The woman is his neighbor's wife, a German immigrant named Helga whom he painted often."

Daniel tilts his head. I see him reading her passive lips, her relaxed eyelids, languid, a woman after sex or a warm bath.

"What do I know?" he says, "I'm not an artist." He pulls in closer to admire the details that render her face. A real person but also a dream. Her lips bow slightly into a secret smile.

* * *

The first line I wrote about Daniel: *I want to flow over your body like water.*

We met in a gym, and every afternoon after work I would watch him. The way his handstand pushups (back to the wall, hands on the floor, heels sliding up and down the sheetrock) fought gravity, the way he threw the barbell up through the hips in the clean and jerk, the way his shoulders finished a long rowing stroke, the way he dipped his baseball cap down and left silently. The way he seemed half shadow made me want to write again. I spent a season rolling his name around on my tongue like a salted stone, sucking on it, keeping it in my cheek.

"I never thought you'd write about that," he says about a piece when it's published, open in his hands, an essay about his body under my hands.

Was it every day? Did he call, or did they brush into each other in the orchards that separated their properties? Wyeth painted Helga outdoors and in the upstairs bedroom of a friend's home down the road where he stashed hundreds of canvases that were only unveiled when they were all purchased by Leonard E. B. Andrews. When the collection was sold, it contained over two hundred works of this one woman, this immigrant woman with her European features that he found so romantic, so hard, and her hair like corn silk. Did she sense when the light was right and then go to him? Wyeth's wife and business manager knew about just a handful of the Helga paintings before they were sold. He kept them secret. Why? The press loved the story, "Legendary Painter Has Secret Blond Mistress/Muse," and his wife never corrected them. The stories made the Helga paintings infamous and drove the price up on all of Wyeth's work. Maybe he was ashamed of his obsession. Maybe he couldn't explain it, how, in this one woman, he saw two hundred works of art.

First in a heavy overcoat, green-brushed felt in the orchards of spring, her hair in girl's braids. Then wearing pants and a man's shirt, walking briskly across the fields. Feel her power, feel the season rising from the ground. And then her great round breasts (she was a mother of three), her pink nipples, and her glittering nest of pubic hair. She lets her hair down. She braids it again. She smiles and reclines on the daybed. She turns away and looks out as the dusk falls over her family's farmland. She stands on her knees in messy sheets, and sunlight paints her stomach, her pelvis, and her thighs.

Wyeth titles his works: *Letting Her Hair Down. In the Orchard. Crown of Flowers. Her Head. Asleep. Nude. Drawn Shade. Overflow. Braids. Night Shadow. From the Back. With Nell* (an old Labrador retriever). *Day Dream. Lovers.*

A critic said that Helga was a young woman taken advantage of by an older, famous painter, that what makes these paintings electric is a naughty sense of *Lolita* sinfulness. I laughed when I read his article. Helga was thirty-eight years old with three children when Wyeth began painting her. Look at her smile. I see it even in his quick sketches. Later, she tells reporters about the noble pursuit of making art, of creating something bigger. His words through her lips.

In college I took life drawing lessons. The light in Portland, Oregon, was always gray, so our studio was lit with bright stage lights. Once a week we'd work from a model. It was exhausting, a four-hour exercise in realism. I'd crack my knuckles; I'd shimmy in my seat. The models would begin to shake and sweat in the stage lights. The first models were half a dozen soft women whose lines I loved tracing with charcoals. How easily breasts and hips flew from a hand, how deep the shadows and bright the highlights! But they seemed to quit mid-semester and were replaced for the remainder of our sessions with the same two male models.

The first, a man with a pregnant lady's belly, walked into the room already naked. He had no need for the demur bathrobe. He brought his own props—costume weapons—and would lunge at us with lances and foils, striking wide-legged poses that caused his fat to jiggle. His genitals would sway back and forth steadily until they hung still between his legs. Too polite to laugh, I tried desperately to avoid his proud gaze. I worked the shadow on his gut for hours one afternoon.

The other model looked like a washed-up rock star. His tattoos were fading to blue, and his skin pulled away from his bones like melting wax. There were deep pockets under his eyes that the stage lights only deepened. When he disrobed he'd turn his back to the class. He was so skinny I could count the bones of his spine. He was impossible to draw: no muscle, no fat, just bone and muddy skin. He draped himself over the daybed like an anemic cat so that I spent more time drawing the furniture and sheets than his form.

The next semester our assignment was to reproduce from a photograph a portrait, at least six feet tall, of our subject's face. I was dating a passionate basketball fan (the Lakers), and in an attempt to find some connection with him during the hours he spent in our apartment watching NBA games, I decided to pick a favorite player and team. I selected Steve Nash, the Canadian point guard for the Phoenix Suns. He didn't seem to belong on the court until he started moving. When he shot free throws he'd stick his tongue out of his mouth and screw down his eyes with concentration. I chose to draw his free-throw face with charcoals on a six-foot piece of paper. Even in that face you could see that he was lean like a soccer player (he'd played soccer in high school), his muscles twisting up with a gooseneck toss of the wrist. I drew his pinched tongue. I sketched his focused eyes. I tried to capture the allure of his athletic gaze, that thing that made me warm for him. Passion. Body. Training. Muscle. All distilled into a frame.

* * *

At boarding school, in our writing center building, there was a great stone fireplace. It looked like something from a hunting lodge. In the winter a gas fire snapped behind iron grates, and I'd sit by it on the carpeted floor, close enough to escape the cold of winter in Northern Michigan. The fireplace was called the Muse, and she could be turned on and off with a remote control. On. Off. I laughed at the notion that inspiration could be turned on and off so automatically. I stared into those blue fires and got lost.

All the writers I loved at that time—Jim Harrison, Hemingway, Rick Bass, Norman Maclean, James Dickey—were older men who loved to fly fish and hunt, and I despaired at being a lean, moody teenage girl, the sort of nymph that would have caught their eye, perhaps a muse but not a writer.

* * *

The female muse: I think of *Venus de Milo,* with her arms gone, unable to hold you or push you away. I think of *The Winged Victory of Samothrace,* Nike, goddess of victory, who is left now with only breasts and wings open to a sea breeze, no face or limbs. Her arms and head have never been found, but in 1950 a team unearthed her missing right hand. Fingerless, it was discovered under a rock near where she had originally stood. In the Kunsthistorisches Museum of Vienna, the goddess's ring finger and thumb were discovered in a storage drawer and taken to the Louvre where they are now displayed next to her in a glass case with her severed hand. A woman in pieces. I think of Apollo chasing Daphne, his lust driving her to transformation. As he touched her, the pink skin of her buttocks turned to twisted wood, her long hair became rigid twigs, her lips sealed up to a scar seep-ing amber sap. She felt a heavy numbness fill her blood and broke upward into bud.

* * *

Tempera is made by mixing distilled water with egg yolk and dry pigments. It has to be applied quickly because it stiffens and dries. Wyeth said, "Tempera is in a sense like building, really building in great layers the way the earth itself was built." He painted Helga in tempera while she was letting her hair down in a sliver of sunlight.

Dry brush watercolor can be painted on rough paper— or on dry or slightly damp paper—with a very fast brush- stroke, or with a brush lightly dipped in paint. Each quick stroke was her braid. Each white eyelash. "I work in drybrush when my emotion gets deep enough into a subject," Wyeth wrote. A painstaking process, wringing out the brush after each stroke. Bending the medium from wet to dry, slowing down time. Wyeth had studied and greatly admired Winslow Homer, whose swift watercolor strokes captured waves with one blue streak, clouds with a splash of gray. The dry brush made watercolor exact, almost painfully rendered. Wyeth fought and wrung and scratched out the lines of her body. Helga with a black velvet ribbon tied around her pink throat, Helga standing before a fall campfire, Helga smiling beneath a crown of flowers she picked from the fields and wove while he watched, Helga resting her full buttocks on a stool, her nakedness round and open near a breezy window, Helga on her knees patterned by sun, Helga sitting in the soft woods of winter beneath an old, gnarled tree, its bark black, its branches scraping sky. Helga in an orchard in a green coat, the buds breaking pink from dark applewood.

* * *

When I was a girl and first in love I asked my boyfriend over and over, "What are you thinking?" I was unsettled by the knowledge that he could inhabit my body so physically yet remain so alien to me. To this day the loneliest moments I can recall were by the side of a lover who seemed distant. "What are you thinking?" was my sketch study; holding out a pencil, I calculated my need to know the measurable distance between myself and the muddy depths of another's private brain.

I have learned that there is tenderness in the unknowable— even in the most familiar faces, the eyes of a woman you've painted a hundred times, the lips of a man who has filled two years of my life. I have known Daniel's sleeping lips, wet lips, kissing lips, lips dry from winter winds, talking lips, bitter lips, but never entirely have I known his mind, the pathways of his memory's gallery, or the reason he dreams sweetly or wakes shaken in the softness of a spring night.

I sketched another lover once in charcoal. He was standing in the morning sun on my balcony in Portland. In the foreground are my terracotta pots of herbs, just greening up in the early spring; in the background the earth slides down to meet the Willamette River and Mt. Hood, a dark pyramid against the sunrise. He's wearing black boxers and looking off to the side, probably figuring out the crossword puzzle he left on the kitchen counter, but who knows. He was always inaccessible to me. When I found the picture years later pressed between the pages of a coffee-table book (in the same way that I once dried wildflowers and later opened the heavy volumes to find only the crumbled dust of summers past), I saw I had only captured the boy I imagined him to be. I had dreamed him into life, though he stood before me, his skin rising into goosebumps as I worked.

* * *

I am writing, always, although sometimes I am only watching, taking notes behind my eyes to later form bodies of prose. Didion wrote that "writers are always selling somebody out." The man who acquired all two hundred pieces of the Helga collection (the largest collection of a single subject in American art history) said, "I consider the relationship between any model and artist to be a professional one of their own making and important only to the finished work of art." He never asked the painter about Helga, who she was to him (though he refers to Wyeth as Andy). All he knows is "that she is a German woman with a proud and close family who worked on a nearby farm." When *Time* magazine ran her portrait on the front cover, journalists flooded Chadds Fords, looking for the mysterious blond mistress/muse of America's favorite painter. The townspeople shook their heads, either out of loyalty to their close-knit community or out of their inability to describe the ruddy-cheeked mother of three who worked part-time as a personal nurse to their elderly parents as a *blond bombshell mistress muse*. Helga didn't like the attention of the press either. Is it in anyone's interest to be divine?

When Helga was fifty-eight, Andrew painted their last work together. She is in the woods with her back turned, walking away. But she never strayed far. Later, near the time of his death, Helga, now in her seventies, moved in with Wyeth and Betsy to care for him. She cleaned his bedsores and changed his sheets. He said, "I have such a romantic fantasy about things, if you don't back up your dreams with truth you have very round-shouldered art." I imagine her worn hands, her practiced manner of turning Wyeth to the left and rocking the sheets out from under him. I imagine her sitting by his side as his breath grew ragged. Maybe there were props in the room that she recognized—a stool, a blanket—maybe the room was stark like most of the interiors he painted.

Then, maybe he looked up and saw her smile lines deepen, the crow's-feet spreading from her eyes, her breasts low on her belly, her braids silver-white like corn silk, the facts of realism. She watched shadows ride his features. She saw as the sun rounded his cheekbones and shone off his high forehead where the skin was stretched and nearly translucent. She noted the texture of the bedding, the gnarled wood bedframe, the eyes in the pine boards, the way the curtains billowed like sails. She drew in her mind the artist on his deathbed and sat beside him as the day darkened and all the good light left the room.

When we were first dating, Daniel came to me late at night. I was staying at a mutual friend's house because I was recently divorced and homeless. Daniel spent his days poring over medical textbooks, preparing for his residency, and he would drive over to see me only when he felt he'd learned enough for the day. First the brush of his headlights down the pine-lined drive. Then his truck tires on fresh snow. I'd hear him kick his boots off at the front door. By the time he'd made it upstairs to the bedroom he'd be stripped of his heavy winter clothing. The floodlight by the garage door, visible out of a big picture window, would illuminate him from behind, wrapping him in hard shadow, breaking over muscles, flowing down the ropes of his legs. He'd walk to me in his briefs, peeling his T-shirt over his head.

There was no affair. Neither Andrew nor Helga ever confessed. Perhaps it was a well-kept secret, but I prefer to think that the love between the painter and his model wasn't worth altering with touch. He kept her at brush-length so that she would remain mysterious, so that her specificity wouldn't pour into him and onto the canvas. Helga seems to me a mirror for Wyeth, a polished surface off which his romantic mind could play. She clearly liked the attention, but why shouldn't she? She is confident in her body, there is no hiding or tucking or making amends for wrinkles or body hair or rolled fat. I think Helga loved herself and was pleased to show off. Pleased to sit in her beauty for an afternoon, draped in netting, pretending to be sleeping like her little girls pretended to keep house in a barn, or filling her face with longing and gazing out at the landscape. Perhaps in another life she would have been an actress, but with Andrew she was only herself. From the fire she tended secretly in her unknowable heart, he transformed her with his paints into all his dream women.

Daniel leads always with his shoulder, whether he's shooting a gun, or trail running, or tracking one of his German shepherds on the trail of a lost person, or holding a door for me, or ironing his dress shirt in the morning with a towel wrapped around his slender waist and his dark hair slick from the shower. I have given up trying to draw him (he refuses), but I catch myself wanting to reach for my charcoals and sketch. I watch him shooting in the backyard, noting how the muscles in his shoulders absorb the kickback from his pistol. I watch his sleeping face when I rise before him in the morning. "I want to flow over his body like water," I wrote when he first appeared in my journals. "I want to do with you what spring does with cherry trees," I text him, quoting Neruda. What is love if not transformation, an art, an act of translating the individual into the universal, a man into a muse or a woman into a laurel tree?

* * *

After circling the gallery we head to the coat check. On our way out, Daniel stops and turns us around to look again at Helga. We agree that it is our favorite piece in the small exhibition. The root of the word *museum* is the ancient Greek *mouseion,* a temple dedicated to the muses, so it is fitting to leave Helga there, smiling like she knows a secret. Outside, the rain has stopped, but the city is still steeped in gray. I watch Daniel's face tense in the wind, his strong shoulder draw up around his jaw. As I reach for him, I am reminded that there is something about him that will always escape me, something that I'll spend my life chasing. I don't expect transformation. But know this: a farmer's wife, a mother, slipped away in the afternoons for a few hours when the light was good, and turning herself into a mirror, became a flame.

GREEN THUMB

My mother tells me that my first word wasn't a word; it was the sound the crows made, *ka-ka-ka,* as they startled out of the community garden in front of my parents' duplex.

My mother likes to tell me things about myself, things she believes are true. She can't read me well, although she has known me longer than anyone else. We've never grown close, as if I was trying to prove that old saying wrong about apples falling near to trees. The two of us stand so far apart that there is neither conflict nor affection between us. I was, she tells me with sorrow, born this way. I never grew into her expectations either, and the ghosts of potential daughters hang in her vision.

"You are just like your grandfather," she tells me. And, "A green thumb skips a generation."

My mother's thumbs are black. She kills even the hardiest houseplants, smothering them with water and plucking away at their crumbling leaves.

Here is a picture of me as a little girl: I am watering a tree that Dad and I dug up from the woods and transplanted in our backyard. It's a picture I drew, or it's a picture on the fridge, I can't remember. We've made a little moat around the sapling, and I'm holding a hose, filling the moat with blue Miracle-Grow water. Dad is resting on his shovel. There is a heart floating somewhere in the sky, maybe near the tree, maybe near my father.

The soil I grew up with is called sandy loam. Just a mile away, where the land falls toward the softened banks of the Connecticut River, the soil is classified as prime agricultural, some of the best in the country. In our backyard, the sandy loam tended more toward sand. Sand in my fingernails, in my socks, in my underwear, in my hair like lice. I didn't need to eat it in a big scoop like my little brother did once; its salt was always on my lips.

I was four years old when we made our first family garden, and even now I remember the smell of mud, deep animal, thaw. The garden was a rectangle at the edge of the yard, just as raw and muddy as the whole property, the fields rough from the mower's tires.

A few summers later, when the grass had grown in and the sawdust had rotted into the soil, crows pecked at our tomatoes and cucumbers. They'd burst out when I ran at them, but they'd sneak back in later, iridescent as oil slicks between the rows.

Crows, I wrote on a wooden sign, stay out! I hammered it near the garden. My parents laughed, but the sign worked. I can't explain it today, but the crows stayed away and never bothered us again.

"You're just like your grandfather," my mother said, squeezing my green thumbs.

These stories build like layers. Drive through the West and see the cut of time through rock. Compressed eons. Volcano, dust, ocean floor, forests, bones of animals, red, black, white-streaked. In our backyard I could dig down to a darker, wetter soil.

There was the story of how I was like my grandfather, but there was also the story of how I was adopted or switched at birth because I was so odd and misfitted to my brothers and sisters, so different from my parents. It was clear that I was some sort of changeling. While my younger brother and sisters are light skinned, I grew darkly tan in the summer, and an olive undertone stayed with me through the winter. I was an edge stalker, like the white-tailed deer that walked at the line between forest and field, whose dark eyes I saw once so close while I lay in the tall grass watching crows.

I stuck my thumb out. It hitched me back to my grandfather, the only one anyone ever said I resembled. I held it and examined its whorls like personal hurricanes.

My grandfather died when my mother was eighteen. A falling tree crushed him as he cut firewood during a frigid Vermont winter. The story goes that it was an old elm, dying from Dutch elm disease, the heart a rotten twist of black wood, frozen into shattering ice crystals, so that it fell opposite the direction it leaned.

During family reunions, on the lawn of our family's dairy farm in the Northeast Kingdom, I liked to break away and look for the stump of the tree that killed him. I felt it was a noble sort of quest and that I would somehow know the tree: it might shine, or sing, or stand out from the other ordinary stumps. High at the top of a dirt road, where the grade crested before falling into shaded maple woods, I found a stump, swallowed by blackberry brambles, that I thought was the one. I stood on it and looked over the purple valley to the blue hills of the Green Mountains, fading into August humidity, and thought I knew something of myself.

I don't know why I've always wondered who I am and where I belong. The feeling has followed me since I was very young, and it's stayed with me even when I've loved where I lived. As a child, I clung to the joke that I was adopted. I don't remember who started it, although it was always there, like a fact that I didn't belong, spinning that narrative out past humor into something like hope.

It's about hope, really. To garden is to start the world anew. Gardening is for fools and romantics. You've got to love the work, not just the fruits. Go to the farmers' market for the fruits; go to your knees for the work. Soil stays in the skin for days; it'll work into your pores. It will mark you. Soil is all the things you are and all the things that were, the stars burst apart and crushed under the mortar of time.

I've always had my hands in the dirt, at farms where I worked, even in little pots of herbs when I lived in cities. The connection I'm trying to make is that soil (and let's say soil because dirt is pejorative) equals identity. Many nights, with my hands still soiled despite my scrubbing, I spread *Leaves of Grass* open on my pillow and read aloud from Whitman, finding in him the religion that I felt when lying and watching crows above the field but couldn't express as vibrantly.

> *I visit the orchards of God and look at the spheric*
> *   product,*
> *And look at the quintillions ripened, and look at quintil-*
> *   lions green.*
>   —Walt Whitman

When Daniel and I first drove up to look at the rental property, it was dark. We'd been hunting for a new home, one outside of the city where we could wake to silence. The place was locked, but we used the flashlights on our phones to navigate. In the dark we couldn't get the dimensions right, yard into pasture, lawn into woods; it was all just a green mess of growth. We stood together, bathed in silence. Smelling leaves, soil, and creek water.

In the morning I drove back up to the house with a key from the realtor. The road was an escape back to where we felt at home, a green cathedral. In the empty halls of the old farmhouse I found bright tiling, urine-colored linoleum, wood paneling, the smell of mothballs and insect bombs, but outside, joyfully, there were ancient oaks, their shade quivering, and pasture and slow cattle in many colors brushing up against ragweed stalks and persimmon trees.

"Here," I said, pacing out the dimension, "here I will start a garden." I walked out the lines and stood planted in the center. Below me the Piedmont Plain. Above and to the west the folded skirts of the Appalachian Mountains.

The first morning in the new house was quiet after Daniel left for work. No music save for the sounds of birds. I looked at myself in new mirrors, seeing if I was any different here, any more whole. A great flock of crows scattered from the oaks at the edge of the field. I opened a new notebook and planned a garden. I'd fill it with all the treasures of summer: jeweled tomatoes, sweet peppers, fresh pole beans, peppery nasturtium flowers, and ruby lettuce. It would grow so high that it could hide me; bending down I would weed in the moist shade of plants as they breathed through their leaves, as they turned sunlight into food.

I dreamed on several pages, listing crops, varieties, and successive plantings, cutting back to fit within the lines of my space. I'd never planned a garden before, only vast farm fields. I had to revise, stuff myself into a smaller box, think in inches not feet, but I knew I needed it, knew I needed this work. When I was done planning, I began to dream of myself in the future, working in this garden. The woman I pictured was relaxed, she walked barefoot on the cool earth, she plucked heirloom tomatoes for her dinner, she was perfectly still in her form as a great tree, knowing where she was going and where she began, rooted in the soil.

"My father always kept a garden, it was our family tradition," Mom told me on the phone. Gardening was part of her seasonal ritual, even if she neither loved the work nor excelled at it. She has shown me pictures of the gardens her father grew behind her family's dairy farm where manure-rich soil produced tall stalks of sweet corn and rambling explosions of summer squash. Each winter my grandfather would plan that garden carefully, order his seeds, edit out varieties from the previous season, and add a few new introductions.

My garden grew up in my notebook on a hot May morning.

That afternoon, as I started to unpack, I found a picture of my grandfather in the bottom of a box. My grandmother had kept it on her nightstand. He couldn't be any older than I was then, thirty maybe. His face is smooth and white. He's wearing small round glasses that make him look like a German intellectual. In different clothing, in a different light, he could be my uncle, his son, they resemble each other so clearly. In another picture he's hugging two maple syrup buckets. Behind him stand two immense oxen bound together by a wooden yoke. He's kneeling for the picture, smiling with pride because, I imagine, the buckets are filled with sweet sap, and all around him the trees are dripping, *ping, ping,* into his other steel buckets, and spring is coming, finally, to the woods of Vermont. Below these two pictures my grandmother framed an image of their dairy barn with a brilliant double rainbow.

He was the youngest of five brothers. The oldest four fought in Europe during World War II while he was forced by his father to leave college and run the farm. I don't really know how he felt about this. Bitter? My mother remembers him as sharp, dark, sarcastic, but I can't be certain. She doesn't understand me well either. Maybe he loved the soil.

Maybe he loved the smell of the dairy barn. Maybe he shared my ox-like love of hard work. I'd love for him to have been very much like me.

A man came with a rust-eaten tractor and tilled up the garden plot while I watched with my hands on my hips, the sun hot on my shoulders. The earth was shockingly red. In my plans, I had assumed that I knew all I needed to know, but the soil told me I was in new country. My blank page was crimson, not snow. With my boot I stomped out the bed paths then followed my marks, mounding soil up one way with my shovel, then another, to create high raised beds with sloping volcanic sides. The clay was heavy and the afternoon sun hot. My hands slipped on my shovel, wet with sweat. I tasted my own salt and the salt of the earth.

When I was finished my backbone felt twisted, and my hands were blistered. I was sunburnt around the edges of my tank top and on the top of my thighs. Sitting under the shade of the oak trees, I nursed a bottle of water and admired the deep shadows cast by my ten high beds. I walked Daniel through them when he came home at dusk, speaking alive the plant dreams I'd written: tomatoes! peppers! beans! I had chosen vegetables that he liked to eat, and I told him how we'd cook them together, how in the fall we'd savor what we'd grown all summer.

That night under the shower's water, I felt raw and emptied, nothing but a sack of blood and bones. I had forgotten this type of exhaustion. *Bone tired,* Mom would say. *Body like a workhorse,* she would say. A beast of the field. The next morning, I spread bags of granulated fertilizer—the ground-up bones, feathers, and blood—then the plants and seeds, tucking them gently into the earth.

Summer is an explosion in the south. My garden sprouted, then filled, then overflowed its rows. With growth came bugs, pests, mysterious diseases that blossomed out of the soil or blew in on the wind. I once knew the name of every visitor to my plants, but these were all strangers. Each day I was turned back early from my work, drenched in sweat and red in the face. I began to think of going to the garden as fighting a losing battle. Fire ants riddled my feet, arms, hands, and legs with white blisters.

As I picked our first cherry tomatoes, I wondered if perhaps I was right all along, perhaps I was a transplant. Daniel and I had been joking about a DNA testing service we'd seen advertised online, and during the hot days of July I sucked on that idea, sweet and cool as an ice cube. A feeling is warm, but science is chilly; it is hard and true, something I could hold up and pass around and assay.

I felt guilty ordering the test but also excited, nervous but hopeful. It seemed like the right time to know for certain, since I was in a place of strangeness, each day learning, each day being shocked to find a new bug, this one with legs shaped like elongated spades, sucking on my tomato skins, this one a huge hornet that flew at night into my screens. I wanted, needed, straightforward answers. The test seemed like a chance to know the end of the story I'd been telling for twenty years. I'd be able to know who I was.

By the first week of August, we'd harvested the largest watermelon I'd ever grown. Daniel held it, appraising its weight in the bright sun: thirty pounds? I took a picture of him kneeling in the garden, cradling the watermelon on his knee, smiling proudly. He passed it to me, and it was warm on the top and cool on the bottom where it had lain pressed to the earth. We cut the fruit into huge smiles and sucked the flesh from the rind, spitting seeds into the white farmhouse sink, our elbows dripping pink juice.

When the DNA testing kit arrived, I found the box small like a gift of jewelry or European chocolates. Inside, the papers were thick and the vials had been taped and printed to look laboratory issue, medical grade, the green of the company's vining leaf logo connecting one history to another. I set the kit on the table. The dogs were watching the sunrise in the yard. Bluebirds dried their wings on the clothesline. I wondered at all the things I'd touched that morning.

There was red dirt under my nails from moving the sprinkler in the garden. There was dew on my toes. So much contact: my hands held memories of dog, teapot, sheets, hose, doorknobs, sandals, fork, watermelon rinds, eggshells, tea leaves, cup handle, and faucet. Inside my mouth: watermelon flesh, split under the knife blade and thick with big black seeds, black Indian tea, yellow eggs from my friend's chickens. I had kissed the dogs on their foreheads. Before Daniel left for work, I kissed him too. Would brushing my teeth help? Would his DNA show up in mine? I waited thirty minutes as the instruction required, so this evidence would fade from my taste buds.

Wagging my tongue around my mouth, I washed up enough spit to fill the sample vial to its bold green line. It bubbled and then settled, slightly gray and tepid. I taped my number to the plastic and slipped it into a mailing packet. The dogs followed me down to the mailbox. The neighbor's cows were already standing in the creek, in the shade of the oak and blackberry, crows circling the oak angrily, roosting then bursting into flight. I tapped the mailbox as a wake-up call to the mud wasp that lived underneath. He rose, dragging his thin, red legs above my head, buzzing with irritation. I slipped the packet in, and the wasp returned home, into the spit mud tunnel between the metal and the wooden post.

A few weeks later I opened the results of the DNA test on my laptop, my heart buzzing between my ribs. I scanned the graphics quickly; they'd matched my spit sample to European countries, to Ireland and England, but most importantly they'd matched my sample to one taken by my second cousin, whose name appeared in the corner next to an icon of her smiling face. I was surprised to see her there, as if she'd appeared at my door with no invitation, confirming that I wasn't adopted.

The answer was neither sad nor exciting, not the sort of thing I wanted to end this story.

I think I was really looking for a disconnect more than a connection, or an excuse for feeling what I'd always felt. But the test proved, at least, that my sense of isolation wasn't genetic. I texted Daniel and told him the results. No story, I wrote. Nothing solved or really learned at all. I had relieved myself of the ability to daydream.

I had often fantasized about finding my real family, and I write this with discomfort because I love and have always loved the family I grew up in. My childhood was filled with dress-up games of the lost child, homeless then found by her rightful people. It was easier to claim unbelonging than my more complicated personality and histories, and, after all, what a great story I'd write about all this, with the sort of arc and completion that is so hard to distill from memory. Its plot would rise and fall and rise again instead of progressing, as my story did, as a messy, many-braided history containing me and all I've ever been told about who I am and who I come from.

In the garden that afternoon, in the heat, I let my brain drift and dream of braiding because a braid is how I imagined my genetic data. I admit that I don't fully understand genetics, or what exactly the test proved, but I could visualize DNA as the double-helix model I'd been shown in high school biology class. In the garden, my mind and body separated. Sometimes I thought I could actually see myself from outside my body. I smelled myself. Sweat. Salt. Skin. Hair sizzling.

I dreamed of braids and salt and stars. When my sisters and I were young, our mother braided our hair before church and for school picture days. We share the same thick, healthy hair in different shades (blond, brown, and my reddish-brown), hair that doesn't taper at the ends; rather our braids stay wide until they are tied off at the tip. Mom would French braid single or double braids and finish them with bows and ribbons. The pleats would stay tight all day and only slip in sleep, so we'd wake with halos of stray strands falling down our necks, looping over our foreheads and ears. There is a picture of us, sleepy, cuddled on the couch on a Christmas morning, in flannel nightgowns and loose braids, holding each other. Do I look so different from them?

I spoke out loud to the plants. That summer my voice was often my only companion during the day, and when I spoke, my lips tasted of dust and salt. Some people, like my brother, are driven to eat soil; it drives them to take scoops and nibbles and big bites of it, in longing, I have always imagined, for the heady rush of minerals. Here, the sting of iron, the hard taste of clay. But we are all soil, really. Dust to dust. I once thought of getting those words tattooed on the inside of my arm. The curse of exile from Eden.

> *In the sweat of thy face shalt thou eat bread, till thou return unto the ground; for out of it wast thou taken: for dust thou art, and unto dust shalt thou return. (Genesis 3:19)*

My mother tells me all the things she knows about me that she believes are true.

Maybe the simplest answer is that she's right.

You were always difficult. You liked to be alone.

You had a dark sense of humor, just like your grandfather.

A green thumb skips a generation.

Your first word was ka-ka-ka, *the sound the crows made.*

Late in the summer, the garden was past saving, although it continued to produce wild fruits, hidden in vine and weed. I tended to it anyway. In my garden I was the only woman; my story began there and moved where I wanted it to move as the sun went down. I sat long into the darkening night and watched the fireflies flash in the undergrowth, imagined speaking love phosphorescently, in a binary code.

The moon rose huge and golden over the pasture. It was so bright that I could see the bean plants, the tomato stakes, the cows in the field glowing under the strange light, casting fair shadows. It was a spooky thing, the call of this moon. I stripped off everything except my leather gardening gloves and work shoes.

Cicadas churned out their love songs from the oak forest. By moon and firefly glow, I bent down and pulled out clumps of grass, my skin alive to the night, feeling each flying insect, each breeze. I tucked my body under bushy pole beans, I brushed my bareness against plants and flowering marigolds whose sharp perfume electrified my skin. In the moonlight, I saw myself for what I was. I could have been plant or animal, clay or stardust.

ON HARVESTING

Red stems, *write bulbs,* green spears of leaves, *write brush.* Thick black loam pierced through, lifted from the floor by sunward rising. I with dark spade cut, pry, leaning body weight into handle. Pull up white-haired roots, a delicate sound, the fabric of the known world rupturing. You shear, snipping up the bulb head, gathering the cut roots in your lap for replanting, returning what we can from what we take. Clean knife steel against a mossy boulder, I strip the spade of caked earth, bag our reap. How many seasons have the wild ramps gone unnoticed, growing as all things do with only their star in mind? Is our hunger harder this year, or am I only more driven outward into wild places? These hours cleaned by our promise, reaching for one more season, a star called survival. There is such newness to these days, but then our love is never the same, you, me, both grow quick enough to slip skins. Our ramps, stripped of translucence in the sink. How to say *blistered*? How to say *fried, fresh*? How to know poison from sweetness, wildness? Slivered bright green, mix with beaten eggs, spear on a second-hand fork's silver, slip between your lips, that tongue, those teeth, that beloved well, where words pool, rise up, *forage, find, feast.*

POLISH

I have been focusing on my feet recently because they have been aching and causing me to walk carefully, rolling inward on my big toe and stepping onto the balls to avoid crushing my tender heels. For the past fifteen years I have chosen professions that demand strength and endurance as well as hours of walking or standing, and I think that my feet are finally tired of it all. When I managed an organic farm, I'd often cover eight miles a day trekking down the long rows of vegetables. I jumped in and out of trucks, kicked implements onto tractors, soaked my shoes and socks in dew and irrigation, suffered stings, bites, and cuts, went barefoot, steel-toed, and rubber-booted through humid New England summers and freezing winters. I was younger then and thought little of my feet. When I did acknowledge pain, it was often in a redemptive fashion, and I felt better for having suffered a bit. I liked my living a bit hard around the edges.

The past few months have been busy at the gym where I train people to lift weights, climb ropes up to the high ceiling, pull their chins over bars, and kick upside down onto a wall to perform handstand pushups. Beyond the obviously physical demands of coaching CrossFit—for instance, performing any of these movements on cue to my clients—there is the simple, unglamorous job of standing on my feet for hours. The shoes I wear in the gym are designed to lift and sprint in, not to stand on concrete flooring for half a day. When I come home at night, it isn't my biceps or quads that I massage, but my toes.

There are twenty-six bones in each foot, fifty-two total—one quarter of all the bones in a human body. Some of them are no bigger than a kernel of corn. There are long and short bones, bones shaped like pyramids, and bones like spoons. All stacked up and arranged neatly, they are tasked with supporting my weight as I move through the world. They absorb shock, gravity, jumping, and tiptoeing, and they cushion and generally hold me upright.

As soon as I get my feet on the ground, we say to mean feeling ready. *Grounding* is a term used by yogis that implies the same thing. I am deeply in need of feeling connected and stable. When my feet ache, the discomfort is more than a physical pain; it becomes a sort of spiritual sore, a depression caused by my bone and fiber, which radiates upward. "I feel lost," I said a few nights ago to my boyfriend as we ate a late dinner. "What am I doing with my life?" I had my feet up on a chair, resting them for the first time all day. "You do so much," he replied. "Too much," I said.

When you get to a new place, get a pedicure, my yoga teacher preaches. *Vacation, work travel, moving across country, visiting relatives back in your hometown . . . get a pedicure. It will ground you.*

My boyfriend's parents recently biked along the Camino De Santiago in Spain and sent us pictures of pilgrims wrapping up their bloodied feet. They described their bare feet on the rocks, bruised, bloody, and dusty. To hurt one's feet is a form of penitence.

And, behold, a woman in the city, which was a sinner, when she knew that Jesus sat at meat in the Pharisee's house, brought an alabaster box of ointment, And stood at his feet behind him weeping, and began to wash his feet with tears, and did wipe them with the hairs of her head, and kissed his feet, and anointed them with the ointment. (Luke 7:37–38)

A woman washed Jesus's feet then rubbed them dry with her long dark hair. Caring for the feet is devotional. But I am not interested in the feet of saints; I am interested in my own. Under boots, sneakers, dirt, and sweat, they remain painted and pedicured. Under weight and miles they retain their high arches and long toes, which, when bared or slipped into heels, are sweetly feminine.

By a certain age, I had been taught by my mother to care for myself, to shave my legs and apply makeup, to blow-dry my hair and to stand up tall. I remember the leg-shaving instruction very clearly. Our family was on vacation in Prince Edward Island, and I wore my bathing suit as I sat on the edge of the tub, running a razor from my ankle to my knee as she oversaw the process. That afternoon I got my ears pierced, picked out a pair of gemstone earrings from a jewelry store, and received my own pink razor. I felt intensely feminine and grown up, but I was only eleven. I was hungry for more, but the lessons ended there that day. I don't remember my mother showing me how to walk in high heels or keep dark lipstick inside the lip line. And although we had nail polish in the house and my mother religiously trimmed, oiled, and painted her nails every Sunday night, I don't remember being shown how to perform a manicure or pedicure for myself. Perhaps I learned by watching her.

My mother prefers polish in shades so natural that they could be her own nails. *Subtle,* she calls them, and she owns a collection of thinly tinted polishes that are achingly similar. She is a nail biter and a cuticle puller, and I think that she must keep them that short and that subtle to hide her nervous shredding. When I was a girl I nibbled at my nails too, and I remember a polish my mother applied to rid of me of that habit. It tasted bitter and smelled like medicine, so I learned to keep my fingers out of my mouth. My mother considered nail biting a nasty habit, though she picked at hers privately.

I learned to paint my nails first with that bitter polish, then with sparkling shades from the drug store. Nail painting was something I did at home, and I was surely an amateur. My young hands smeared paint on my skin, spilling over the breach of my cuticles. Although I held paintbrushes often, the tiny nailbrushes were awkward and my close-cut nails poor canvases. Anyone who has attempted the feat knows that one hand will look smoothly applied and the other, painted with your nondominant hand, will look a mess. Too much polish will flood. Not enough will streak and appear sheer. I tended to paint heavily, a Van Gogh of polish, as if the nails were concepts, not countries with distinct boundaries.

In northern New England, where I grew up, feet were often hidden and thus secretive, but in Malibu they were a public display of the care a woman invested in herself. I had my first spa pedicure when I moved to California, where feet should always be pretty. It was my first exposure to the culture of self-improvement. My sister had experimented with home hair dyes in high school, and at that point I had two small tattoos, but I had never thought of beauty as a curated, everyday experience. I'd done my makeup for special occasions, school dances, and trips to see the ballet in Boston, but never on a regular schedule.

I don't remember the specifics of that first pedicure, partly because nail salons are universal spaces and partly because I was never able to pinpoint where I was in Los Angeles in relation to anything else. I imagine that the salon was in a one-story strip mall, the type that line Ventura Boulevard and many other American streets. And if I was to say whom I went with, it was likely my ex-boyfriend's mother and sister, and perhaps one of her beautiful, messy teenage friends.

We sat beside each other in a row of massage chairs, and while our backs and breasts vibrated, we sank our feet into a warm bath. What I learned during that first pedicure was that it was a silent exchange. Sometimes there will be a water feature trickling in the corner, or a flat screen playing muted CNN, or a family talking over takeout in the back, but the technician, whoever she may be, will say almost nothing to you. She will, however, speak to her fellows, either casually with the person working next to her or yelling at the kids in the back. Ninety percent of nail salons in the US are owned and operated by Korean Americans, and since I don't understand Korean, I am always terribly self-conscious. I flip through an out-of-date magazine or scroll through my phone to avoid this language barrier, as a stranger silently begins to clean my feet.

Consider that most cultures have foot-reading traditions. Consider that a foot will flatten, curl, and bruise depending on how you use it. Consider your hair, your tattoos, your flaking polish, your dry skin, and then presenting it to another person, usually another woman. The first thing she'll do is look over your feet as if assaying the task. Prior to that first pedicure, I had been working at an organic farm where I was often barefoot in muck and manure, and when I'd come to Los Angeles, my feet were tough and callused enough to walk on hot blacktop. The technician must have filed and scrubbed them with stones and tools that resemble small-toothed cheese graters until they were smooth.

With an orangewood stick she must have cleaned out my cuticles and then buffed my nails shiny, all while cars passed silently, the chair vibrated, and the magazine lay limp on my lap. I don't remember what color I had painted during that first pedicure or if we ever returned to the same salon. I recall only the silence, but for the sound of water, and the openness, that act of baring myself to a stranger. It was something I began to long for, like confession.

As I write this, my toenails are painted a deep purple because I have been listening to the music of Prince, and that color, the color of royalty, is his. It's a personal tribute. I have chosen toenail colors in protest, in longing, in joy, in jest, and in rebellion. Color is that capstone of emotion; it has its own language as subtle and vast as literature. Color is essential to the care of my feet; the rainbowed wall of choices at a salon helps me divine my mood. Jewel toned or tropical, neutral or neon, holiday themed or matched to a dress, these shades are personalities; even their names are fantasy: Big Apple Red, I'm Not Really a Waitress, Russian Navy, The Tasmanian Devil Made Me Do It.

Why ornament the lowest extremity? The body part that holds me to the earth? Why not treat feet like the workhorses they are, practical and prone to dirtiness, stink, and sweat? I was not always so bold. I felt confined to binary definitions of tough/girly, gritty/pretty, strong/sexy for most of my twenties, painting my toenails late at night, drunk on wine and with abandon. During the day I kept my painted toes a private affair, unable to articulate why I could work so hard and get so dirty and then delicately paint my nails light pink. Under my steel-toed boots I could feel them, shamefully feminine. At some point I decided there was enough ugliness in the world to afford the luxury of painted toes. I could be both dirty and dolled up.

Babylonian soldiers painted their fingernails and toenails before battle. They were buried with solid gold manicure kits and pots of pigment alongside their weapons and armor. Brides in India stain their hands and feet with henna. Egyptian soldiers did up their nails to match their lips, both red as blood. Queen Nefertiti's nails were ruby while Cleopatra's were crimson. During the Ming Dynasty, only the nobility could polish their nails red and black, leaving all the other shades to the common people.

Bright color is rare in nature and is challenging to stabilize and make use of as a pigment or dye. For much of history, bright colors were reserved for religious and royal objects.

How do you see an azure butterfly and not want that color for yourself? In a mostly green and brown world, how could you not envy the parrot, the bluebird, the coral beneath the waves? Take beautiful things and roll in them. Paint the most brilliant shades of nature on your skin.

Dolly Parton recalls her first poor-girl's makeup kit. "Until I was a teenager," she said in a magazine interview, "I used red pokeberries for lipstick and burnt matchsticks for eyeliner."

Ancient nail polish was made by mixing color into egg whites, beeswax, or pastes. Pigments and paint grinders have been found in a cave in Tanzania dating from 350,000 years ago. In nature, bright color can be extracted from a variety of things, including snails. The Murex snail produced Tyrian purple, a dye so precious that its manufacturing was guarded by successions of dynasties. Its shade became the color of royalty, a king's gown edged in ermine, the velvet of a crown's backing, and later, using synthetic dyes, the flamboyant signature suits of the artist Prince. Ground-up, semiprecious stones, like lapis lazuli, created jewel tones. Soils like the burnt dirt from Sienna, Italy, made oranges and tans. The crushed bodies of parasitic insects from Central America, cochineal bugs, were responsible for giving the cardinals of Europe their red robes and English soldiers their distinctive uniforms.

In organic life, color is an evolved mechanism. It can serve as warning or invitation, war paint or makeup. Being able to see a wide range of color is useful for omnivores, like human beings. Women can typically distinguish more colors than men, especially in the red and pink ranges. I've read that this was probably the result of natural selection: the women who could gather the ripest fruits (and the fewest underripe or toxic foodstuffs) were most successful. I can look out my window and tell which persimmons are turning perfectly soft by their sheen and shade alone.

Nature contains the beauty I covet. As a girl I boiled purple cabbage to make purple dye for my white T-shirts. I gathered the most scarlet of the fallen maple leaves and pressed them between wax paper. I collected bluebird feathers and robin eggshells. My own body—brown, red, pink—was so bare, I thought, bathing in the brook that ran through our backyard in the dabbled shade, that I could imagine myself animal, camouflaged in that landscape. I wanted more, in a secret, almost shameful way. I wanted red like the blood trails I'd follow on fresh snow, neon green like the buds in spring, the orange of a sky before a thunderstorm, and the metallic black of a crow's feather.

But what I wanted most of all, and still can hardly describe, is sparkle. I was forbidden to use glitter in my art projects as a girl since those small plastic flecks polluted everything in the house, eyelashes, clothing, the cat's fur. Even to say *glitter* seems to cheapen its glow, lowering it to the level of kitsch. When I select a nail polish with a shimmer, or shine, or glitter, my fingers and toes take on the same light-shattering power as fresh snow, sunlight on water, dew droplets suspended from a spider's web, stars in the darkness of a wilderness night. This sparkle, this breaking, is the opening of one color to all colors, it is movement too. When my nails are painted with glittery polish, I signal to joy, like a mirror flashing code; I call it down with a mimic's flattery.

This morning I propped my feet up on the windowsill. They are still sore, but the ache is less specific, a kind of homesickness of the sole that allows me a moment to stare at my own toes as the sunlight flares through them.

I don't think that I've ever looked at my own feet so closely. In life drawing class, I stared at a model's feet for so long I couldn't help but see them as hands grasping at the folds of a draped blanket. Feet and hands share many of the same bone structures, save the complexity of the heel and the strength of the opposable thumb. Staring at my feet, I can make my brain flip and see fingers instead of toes. The more I look, the stranger they become.

I begin by massaging my feet to get the ache out. A communicating nerve in the foot has to send a message a long way to the brain. Sometimes these messages get muddled. Feet are easily sexualized in that they are intimate and concealed. In high-heeled shoes the toes press together, forming a miniature image of a women's cleavage against the vamp of the shoe. A website recommends that you reveal just a bit of toe cleavage, since too much is too sexy. Searching for sexy feet online yields pictures of feet very much like mine—long, high arched, with well-kept nails—as well as video clips of high-heeled feet stepping easily on eggshells and birthday cakes, produced for fetish viewing.

In attempting to explain the foot fetish and the general sexiness of feet, neurologist Vilayanur Ramachandran proposed that the feet and genitals are connected through the somatosensory cortex and that those individuals who are highly aroused by feet experience some sort of crosstalk between the part of the cortex responsible for feeling feet and the part of the cortex tasked with feeling the more traditional between-the-legs erotic zone. His study concludes with a reference to amputees reporting experiencing orgasms in their missing feet, a distraction greater, I imagine, than my sore heels.

There is something essential about feet; maybe it's their similarity to hands or to the fins and paws of other mammals; maybe it's their commonality and their utility that can render them into bodies in miniature. They are small visions of our physicality. Reflexology connects each part of the foot to a corresponding body part. The big toe is paired with the pituitary gland, throat, nose, and cervical spine; the heel with the glutes and lower back; the mid-foot with the kidney; the ball of the foot with the lungs. Each foot mirrors its side of the body, which is actually very similar to how the somatosensory cortex organizes tactile representation. The cortex is arranged in an orderly but inverted fashion from left to right and up to down, starting at the top of the cerebral hemisphere with the big toe and ending with the mouth at the bottom of the cortex. A body part's region in the brain is not related to its actual size on the body but to how much we can feel from it. Thus the hands and feet have the greatest representation in the cortex.

The skin on the soles of our hands and feet is different from the skin anywhere else on our bodies. This glabrous skin lacks hair and pigmentation and contains the highest concentration of sweat pores, which is why, when we are nervous, we suffer from sweaty palms and clammy feet. The glabrous skin on the feet is the body's thickest because it has to bear the weight we continually place upon it. This pressure also creates the calluses that are filed off during a pedicure, leaving the feet smooth again. But despite the thickness of the skin, I can almost see side to side through my mid-foot as it is backlit by the sun. I can count its bones, the long ropes of veins, the solid form of my nails.

My nails look quite nice displayed against the morning light. The polish is still slick and unbroken. My second toe is longer than my big toe, a proportion called *le pied grec,* one of the few things I remember from fourth-grade French class because I recall staring at my foot, bravely unsocked, and feeling proud for having such a long second toe. This "Greek foot" is supposed to signify a personality that is creative, ambitious, sporty, responsible, but rather inclined to perfectionism and control. I might remember that French class because this foot reading so accurately describes my character. I don't put stock into horoscopes, but I do notice when they seem to align well.

I pull up a foot-reading website and read that I am, according to Astrogle.com, a solid worker, independent, self-sufficient, occasionally antisocial, expressive, and adventurous. Or that is what my feet say, reading from their width, arches, and arrangement of toes. I wiggle my last toe independently; that

that little baby of a toe can move on its own is proof that I am
both rebellious and good in bed. I appreciate my feet speaking
so well of me despite what I make them endure.

The press of my foot to the earth springs a hundred
*   affections,*
They scorn the best I can do to relate them.

—*Walt Whitman*

My feet hold memories of knife blades, rocks, clamshells,
nails, bees, and hoes. They recall the confines of a wet boot
in August heat and the freezing numbness in December when
even two layers of wool socks couldn't keep winter out of the
bone. They remember a night in New Orleans when I bought
a new pair of flats in the French Quarter and broke them in
by walking around with a bottle of rum until my heels bled,
and then I walked barefoot. In the hotel bathtub, my feet were
almost black from the blood and street. They remember the
fur of my childhood dog, who I used to massage with my toes.
But they remember most vividly the pedicures they've been
treated to as I attempted to ground myself and grow.

The process of a pedicure requires several of the qualities
that I strive for. It requires trust, patience, humility, and still-
ness. In vibrating massage chairs, my body jiggles and knocks
against itself and the chair. The hours in a salon move differently than they do elsewhere, so that *People Magazine* from
two years ago still seems relevant and forty-five minutes of
scrubbing, massaging, clipping, and painting feels necessary,
not indulgent.

The pilgrim on the Camino de Santiago has made a choice
to batter her feet. She has decided to suffer. I am trying, more
every year, to choose comfort.

Get off a plane in Olympia, Washington, in cool rain drizzle, too early to meet the boy you are tragically in love with; he is still in class. Go to the mall. Waste hours there. Go to the salon and have your nails painted a hopeful pink, and then wait for him in your rental car, in the pouring rain, outside of the apartment complex where he no longer lives, and know, even before he ducks into the passenger seat and you head to the motel room, that this trip will not be what you'd hoped.

A year later, still heartbroken, on a dark night before Christmas, get a pedicure no one will ever see under all the boots and socks of New England's December. Sparkling like golden snow on your toes, the color is your secret all holiday season when you are so lonely that you could hug a stranger just for the touch of it. It feels so lovely to have your feet touched that you set the magazine down and just watch the technician perform her rituals.

Get a pedicure with your college friend before her wedding, a marriage that feels ill-fated already, and together polish yourselves beautiful and shimmering in the silence of a salon.

Get your nails done alone before your own doomed wedding, a neon pink mani-pedi that fits neither your wedding colors nor your dress but instead screams "freedom!" like Mel Gibson in *Braveheart*.

Have your nails painted before your sister's wedding with your mother and younger sister. The four of you—your sister who is the bride, your sister who isn't, and your mother—sit in silence as the polish dries. *Is this what it means to be family? Are we creating our own female rituals?* you wonder. Your nails are mint green. Your mother's, as usual, are so nail-colored they don't look painted.

Get a pedicure after your divorce with a color called "longshot."

Get a pedicure when you move to a new state.

When you are stuck in an airport flying to Iceland, get your toes painted the color you imagine the water in Iceland will be (it is).

Get a pedicure on your afternoon off, in the mall, and finally, finally feel the weight leaving your feet. Let the color be purple for Prince, whose song "My Name Is Prince" starts with a sound as close to a sparkle as a sound will ever get.

ON REVISION

Two things happened. They were unrelated, but because revising abstract chunks of reality into something understandable is the genesis of most narrative, these two things united into a story.

1

The auxiliary port that allowed me to attach my phone to the sound system of my Honda burned up in a quick copper flash, so I went to Walmart and dug though the five-dollar CD bin for driving music. A two-disc best-of album, *Prince4Ever,* took up slots five and six of the CD player's buttons, and I touched them slowly, hesitantly, first humorously, then with a near pornographic fascination until I couldn't get enough and the soundtrack of my life shifted abruptly, taking a neck-breaking tonal shift to funk and sex and long guitar licks.

+ 2

I realized one morning while checking my bank statement online that I had enough money in my savings account for breast augmentation, a surgery I had yearned for since my breasts stubbornly refused to grow much larger than clementines during adolescence. I savored the idea of breast augmentation, I laughed at it, I let it grow into excitement, a phone call, a consultation, and finally a date for surgery, which I would come to describe as a birthday gift to myself and a revision of a form that I long held as out of order with its truth.

=

Prince became the soundtrack of my breast augmentation. I wouldn't be able to listen to anything while I was having my breasts operated on, but on the drive over to the clinic, before the sun came up, as my Honda slipped through the dark roads and waking subdivisions of northern South Carolina, I played "Peach" and "Purple Rain" and waited, eagerly, for what came next, the moment when I would be reborn as myself.

* * *

Most readers who look closely at Whitman's revisions soon realize that while some may help, most do not, and many harm the poems, often severely. . . . I came up with a solution. I took as my starting point what I regard as the most satisfactory version of each poem (usually, but not always, the earliest version). I then compared it with all other versions. When I found a distinctly superior reading—some happy rewriting or blessed deletion, or in the case of a superseded version, an abandoned felicity—I incorporated it into the version at hand. Some of the poems in this book, therefore, are in versions that have never before existed.
—Galway Kinnell,
on how he edited Whitman's poems for
The Essential Whitman

* * *

It was a routine examination, a yearly ritual. How many times had I bent forward with my shirt pushed up over my head as a school or camp nurse walked their fingers over my spine looking for a curve before one of them caught it? A subtle shift, first toward my ribs and then off to the left, thirteen degrees, like a curse, like a flag waving in a slight breeze, but the fabric was my bones and my body stood just lopsided enough to raise one shoulder and one hip. But I bent just one degree away from being diagnosed officially with scoliosis.

"The good news is you won't need treatment," my orthopedic specialist said when I was fifteen. She was studying an X-ray of my spine and pelvis against a wall of light. I sat on the crinkly paper of the exam table trying to look over her shoulder at the image of my insides. She didn't say what the bad news was, but her first statement's negative contained it. No treatment meant no improvement, no help, the occasional chiropractic correction maybe, but consistent low-level pain forever. My pain scale is skewed, I think, from this consistency.

I knew that it was my final appointment with this specialist, a well-dressed, sexy woman, the sort of woman that, at fifteen, I longed to have contact with. She seemed successful, exciting, and powerful. She bound her long dark hair with silver chopsticks. Her lipstick was bright and perfectly outlined so that even up close it never smudged, and she wore heels that made her sound like a storm trooper marching down the tile hallways of the hospital. After this appointment I'd return to the matronly care of our family doctor, whose husband was my high school English teacher and whose children were learning to play the piano from my mother and who felt, like many women in my small hometown, more like my mother's confidant than my own.

She left my X-ray hanging on the light board and sat down in a swiveling chair by my knees. Writing out the name of a chiropractor, she asked, "Any questions?"

It seems in retrospect a silly question, a trivial one for a woman who was diagnosing me with untreatable lifelong discomfort, but perhaps not; perhaps I knew then that some things hurt more than bones and muscles. "Are my breasts going to get any bigger?"

She looked again at my X-ray and pointed with her pen at the cup of my pelvic bone. "Probably not. Your bones are

already fused, which means you are pretty much done growing." I had arrived at my final form.

I remembered a checklist our fifth-grade health class
received of all the signs to expect through puberty: underarm
air, pubic hair, acne, menstruation, weight gain, and breasts. I
was done with that. The body I was sitting in was my grownup
body, bent, with one cocked shoulder, one drooping hip, and
small breasts. She must have sensed my heartbreak because she
pulled up close to me, and I saw her well-lined lips and smelled
her clean perfume and she smiled a big, friendly, woman-to-
woman smile, not a kid's smile, and I felt at once proud to be
old enough to be friendly with her and proud to be a woman.

"You never know," she said, grinning. "My sister had
small breasts when we were teenagers, and every day, on the
way back from school, she'd stop at the church and light a
candle and pray to Mary for bigger ones."

"Did it work?" I asked. Her eyes drifted as she must have
remembered that church of her youth, and I imagined it was
one of those dark, stone-cold Catholic beauties with primary-
colored stained glass spilling neon sunlight over crucified
Jesus and sweet Mary in periwinkle robes above the flickering
candle of a teenage girl who, with folded hands, her knuckles
pink from the cold, asked the Mother of God to please grant
her a great rack.

"It worked. She's wears a D cup now, much bigger than
me, but I never prayed." Smiling still, the doctor flipped closed
my file, pushed her chair back to the desk, and flicked off the
X-ray lightbox.

Somewhere in my medical file there is an X-ray of the curve
my spine makes and the date when my pelvic bones fused to
make me officially *a woman,* a day when hope and loss were
mixed up and knotted and my not growing meant my back
could contort no further but also that I would not fill out and
nothing would help me. Despite all this, I was told that prayers
might be answered.

Dearly beloved, we have gathered here today
To get through this thing called life
Electric word, life. It means forever and that's a mighty
*   long time.*

—Prince

When Prince's death was announced online, I was lying in bed, typing. Daniel yelled the news at me from his office, where he was also typing. Later that evening he called me in and said, "Watch this. This is the most rock-and-roll moment I've ever seen," and he pulled up a YouTube video of the George Harrison Rock & Roll Hall of Fame tribute. Stop reading, google it, and check this out now.

Wait for it.

In the first few minutes of the video you might not even see Prince. Tom Petty is leading the band through a faithful cover of "While My Guitar Gently Weeps," which will end up being not a revision but a complete remake of what the band practiced the previous evening when Prince failed to play a solo but promised he'd do something live. Petty is out front, wearing sunglasses that mask how skillfully he's directing everyone. Jeff Lynne, Marc Mann, and George's son, Dhani, are all playing guitar. They look, very simply, like dressed-down rock stars and bluesmen. Marc Mann plays Eric Clapton's original solo soulfully, and then, almost two minutes in, the camera cuts, and if you haven't seen him already at far stage left, just outside the spotlight, strumming carefully, paying attention to his fretwork like an amateur while he plays backup, there's Prince in a bright red hat, a high-collared red shirt under a long black coat with an asymmetrical hem, a leopard-print guitar strap, and a silk handkerchief in his pocket.

The camera moves back to center, but you'll notice Dhani Harrison smile and look to his left, and what you don't see is Prince pushing forward gracefully, the other men melting away, until he's standing in front of Harrison and just to the side of Petty. The spotlight frantically finds Prince, and he closes his eyes like a man paying his respects, then he picks up the intensity, turns to Petty and smiles, then starts in for real. He holds the guitar like he's reloading a shotgun. He quickly raises it to his face and licks the strings. He turns around, exposing his back to the audience, and briefly Petty loses his grin, until he realizes what Prince is going to do, which is jam with him and Harrison while falling backward into the arms of a waiting bodyguard below the stage. Harrison's joy is perhaps the most charming moment of this tribute; he is clearly thrilled to be playing his dad's song on stage while Prince slashes through a solo. The music takes a shift and is suddenly something newly born.

Pushed back on stage, Prince appears to stumble like a man possessed by the Holy Spirit, until he finds his footing, one black, high-heeled boot against an amplifier, and looks over at Petty, who nods. Then Prince's serene face breaks into pure delight, and he lets the music twist him, he throws his head back, he kicks out the hem of his long black coat. Meanwhile, Petty is dutifully leading the band through yet another chorus. Prince finally turns back to the band, pulls his guitar low, and shuts his eyes to enjoy the staggering, drawn-out pleasure of his final notes as the band cools down. As Petty pulls them together with a quick look to all sides, and as everyone closes up, Prince takes off his guitar and throws it straight toward heaven. He walks off stage before the applause, and in the video you can't see his guitar come back down.

"I was there," drummer Steve Ferrone said later. "I saw the guitar go up, but I never saw it come back down."

"Maybe George Harrison caught it," someone wrote in a Reddit thread.

This performance should come up if you search "how to steal the show."

It should make you weep.

My younger sister and her best friend, Meredith, spoke sooth-ingly to their growing breast tissue during high school because they learned in science class that plants respond to such treat-ment. Years later, they both have beautiful, full chests.

When I was seventeen, my boyfriend sent me a link to a website that promised a magic formula that, for only ninety-nine dollars a month, would my increase breast size. There was cruelty on his part, of course, but I can accuse myself only of wistful dreaming. It is one thing to imagine yourself in a new form and another to be pushed there.

I used to visualize the woman I would become as if I might be able to make her materialize out of fantasy. She'd be me, of course, but better. She wouldn't smoke, or drink, or cry nearly as much as I did at sixteen. She'd be a few inches taller, maybe just from standing straighter, for having pulled her spine up by her willpower alone. She'd have the patience to grow her hair long, and it would flow over her breasts so she'd resem-ble the girl from the North Country that Bob Dylan pined for. This revised version shifted to new women as I grew, like a mirage on a desert road rolling out ahead of your car, endless and reflective.

Because I saw the gulf between myself and my future being, and because I wasn't the sort of rock star who could change her name from Robert Zimmerman to Bob Dylan but was instead more like Prince, whose birth certificate reads *Prince* and who had only to grow into a mold, not conjure it and then create the wax too, I ordered the magic formula for ninety-nine dollars a month. The concoction was fennel based and included fennel tea, which I was to drink at morning and bedtime; fennel soap, with which I was instructed to wash my breasts in a circular, massaging motion; fennel lotion, which was to be applied in the same manner as the soap; and fennel capsules, big clear pills that I had to choke down twice a day. The printed material also asked me to abstain from caffeine and sugar during the process and to massage my breast tissue (in addition to the time with the soap and lotion) for ten minutes a day, which felt excessive given the amount of tissue I had to massage.

My skin, breath, sweat, hair, and spit all smelled like fennel, a licorice-sweet bitterness that I despised then and which now brings me back to those long minutes in high school when I tried to coax my body into something for myself and for a boy I thought I loved. Fennel is lovely roasted or shaved raw over fish, but to me it is the taste of futility, scam hopefulness.

* * *

Whitman spent the last part of his life trying to get his book right. He kept working over those old poems, as Lady Gregory said of Yeats, as if he were in competition for eternity. . . . A year before his death, Whitman said, "In the long run the world will do what it pleases with the book." I would like to interpret this remark as indicating acceptance of such enterprises as this attempt of mine to consolidate the best of all his efforts to perfect his finest poems.

—*Galway Kinnell*
on Whitman's life of revision

* * *

It's hard to research Prince because he revised himself constantly; his public persona was so uncomfortable with its publicity that even at his most charming there is something off-putting about his interviews. In her essay "Ceremony of the Interview of Princes," Elena Passarello describes him as looking, in interviews, like a cat wearing a sweater. At his worst he's talking to Oprah about his infant son who has been dead for weeks, but he's denying it. At his best he is flirtatiously shifting his eyes and delivering zingy one-liners, throwing shade at his peers and at the interviewer for having asked him such silly questions. It's hard to figure out who he was, or who he wanted to be.

In his standout performances, he appears shy at first. Watch him cover Radiohead's "Creep" at Coachella, and he wanders around wearing what looks like a pair of white, bejeweled pajamas until he transforms into a guitar god; or the first live recording of "Purple Rain," during which he lets Wendy Melvoin cycle through the intro again and again while he ghosts through the band waiting for his moment; or, during Super Bowl XLI, as he charms his way onto the set, Miami rain pounding the stage, and then strips off his bandana as if he's finally opening up to audience and asks, genially, "Can I play this guitar?" before breaking into a storm of music from his purple axe made in the shape of the symbol that he insisted for a few years be used instead of his name. He seemed always to be shifting. He seemed always to be thinking of the end of the world.

Early one morning in the medieval town of Škofja Loka in Slovenia, I wake before my roommate, a girl in my graduate program traveling abroad with me for two weeks. I don't want to bother her, and the light is so bright already, the church bells ringing. In the streets of the walled city, the bakeries are opening their doors, and here and there a well-dressed man or woman is hurrying off to work. Old men are walking long-haired shepherd dogs, old men are washing the cobblestones with mops, old men are smoking cigarettes in the square as if they've been there all night.

In a narrow street where dawn has yet to walk, where the geraniums and roses hold quivering droplets of dew, I find myself drawn upward toward a shrine. The street rises to it and then stops. Above the shrine is the Church of Mary

Immaculate, the Nuns' Church, and above that the baroque flank of Loka Castle, catching sunlight pinkly. But it is the shrine that pulls me in, because within its dark hollow it is still nightly lit, because Mary's face is so deeply set that the flickering electric candles hardly illuminate her robes and open hands, because, around her hemline, in the cement, gravel, dirt—in the seven hundred-year-old grit—she's been left gifts of Mardi Gras beads, fake roses, votive candles burned down to glass, stuffed animals, wilted geraniums, a tube of lipstick, a few euros.

She is so far away from these things that she seems not to have noticed that years have passed and that so much of what her devotees bring her is false flame and molded plastic. I couldn't touch her, even if I climbed the small gate, my sneakers looped through the ornate ironwork, to try and brush her cheek.

Someone, somewhere, begins to practice the cello, that instrument that breaks even the hardest hearts, soaring like the cry of an electric guitar, legato and slurred, through the silence of the street.

It seems like the right thing to do. Maybe it's the first step.

I kneel on the cobblestone, my jeans soaking up dew, and I close my eyes and hold my hands in prayer and ask, very politely, for beautiful big breasts. I leave her a flower I picked from the hotel's window box, toss it over the fence like a fan throwing a rose onstage to a rock star.

As a teenager I stuffed my bra with toilet paper. I wore a bra filled with gel. But when I took it off, I was as flat-chested as a boy. Sometimes I wore my small breasts like a talisman against overt femininity; they allowed me to express myself, unguarded without overflowing.

I told myself things like: *Amazon archers cut off their breasts to better pull a bowstring close. Zelda Fitzgerald, whose slim athletic figure epitomized style in the 1920s, was flat-chested.*

My small breasts made me bold, but then they also made me shrink from feeling *woman,* especially as I grew and did not become the woman I'd hoped. My sister pulled away my towel as I changed at the beach and laughed at my breasts. My sister giggled at how her dresses fit me. My sister wondered how my future child would latch to my flat chest. My shirts and dresses billowed away from my form and hung shapeless, deflated with disappointment.

What then will be the story I write of myself grown up? We're all told we can be anything we want, and I wanted to be a pediatrician, a wolf biologist, a volcanologist, a storm chaser, a bartender, a farmer, a muse, a poet, a woman, yes, a woman who fit a certain mold, who could be described by hands creating a figure eight in the air, by a certain palm-filling fullness.

On the road through the Julian Alps, a student finally gets the Bluetooth to work on the rental car. We are all tired and leaning against the windows, watching the sunset through clearings where hay is drying on wooden racks and honeybees are circling their hives, when *Purple Rain* blasts through the speakers starting with "Let's Go Crazy," a dance song about the end of the world, then the love songs "Take Me With You," "The Beautiful Ones," and "Computer Blue," in which Prince asks "Where is my love life?" and Wendy Melvoin and Lisa Coleman, his vocalist and keyboard player, sound like they are about to take a warm bath together.

We're onto the Virsk Plain with the walls of Škofja Loka in view when Prince plays "Darling Nikki," and everyone in the van smiles at the image of Nikki in a hotel lobby masturbating with a magazine because *with* is such an odd word choice. Prince cries, begs Nikki to come back, and plays a two-minute guitar solo in honor of her grinding. Then the guitar fades into a gospel chorus singing what sounds like Latin, and we all assume that the words are so dirty that Prince dressed them up like Hail Marys and slipped them in, slyly disguising the carnal as the divine, as was his forte. *What could he be saying?* we wondered.

Later, I read online that those words, which we hoped to be so dirty, are the result of intentional back masking, a mixing technique that plays tracks backward, and instead of singing to Nikki what he'll do to her in the voice of a choir, Prince's chorus is saying, *Hello, how are you? I'm fine, cuz I know that the Lord is coming soon, coming, coming soon.*

I sing the body electric,
The armies of those I love engirth me and I engirth them,
They will not let me off till I go with them, respond to them,
And discorrupt them, and charge them full with the charge of the soul.

Was it doubted that those who corrupt their own bodies conceal themselves?
And if those who defile the living are as bad as they who defile the dead?
And if the body does not do fully as much as the soul?
And if the body were not the soul, what is the soul?
　　　　　　　　　　　—Walt Whitman, "Poem of the Body"

When the surgeon consults on my breast augmentation, he first shows me a computerized image of my future chest, but the graphics look fake, and it's somewhat off-putting to watch him click the plus sign and see my breasts fill up, up, up until I say, "No, not that big," and he clicks the minus sign, and they deflate again. The computer calculates that one breast is two teaspoons larger than the other, a tiny, unflattering unit of measurement, and I wonder whether post-op he'll still record their size in teaspoons or if I will graduate to cups.

I don't like how my body looks on the screen. The image is generated from a picture the nurse took of me early in the appointment, then it's pixilated by the breast-generating program so that it looks falsely, almost spookily, similar to my body. This effect, of created things resembling but not quite capturing the spirit of the real, is called *the uncanny valley effect*. The term comes from a graph created by roboticist Masahiro Mori that plots human empathy against the anthropomorphism of robots. As robots become more realistic, we feel more and more empathy for them and the line on the graph trends upward. But as the robots' humanism approaches that of actual humans, our empathy for them plummets. On the screen, the woman looks similar to me—she has my tattoos, my belly button ring in her navel, my pants on her hips—but her breasts swell to the clicking of a button, and I am startled by her ability to shapeshift. She also seems to magnify my imperfections, her shoulder tilted, one hip lower. I can't stand her asymmetry, her wearing of my skin.

Instead, to give me a better idea of how I might look, the assistant nurse fits me with a bra with empty cups that she fills, incrementally, with gel inserts. Then I slip my T-shirt back over these fake breasts and check myself out in a floor-to-ceiling mirror. At first I get up close and stare only at my boobs, but the doctor recommends that I step back and look at the whole of my body, at its proportions. I blur my vision a bit so that I am just a ghost of a woman's form. I shift side to side, and I see myself in profile and from the front. I ask the nurse for another insert, what will, in surgery, amount to only twenty-five additional cubic centimeters of saline per breast but will take me from a box to an hourglass shape when I look at myself straight on.

I take selfies in the exam room wearing the gel bra, which I will gaze at later during the five months between consult and surgery. I'll show them to Daniel, who encourages me to attain the shape I've dreamt of, cautiously and with guarded excitement. I'll mark them as my favorites so I can find them easily and can see myself as I have always envisioned my body. A slight change and I am that woman.

Prince described the meaning of *Purple Rain* as the sky (blue) mixing with blood (red) at the end of the world. He told interviewers that wanted to get closer to God, to work in the Flow, to write a song every day. He built a house with a vault where he could store those songs. It's hard to read shifts in his career, but it seems that after he created a home for himself at Paisley Park, after the success of *Purple Rain,* he became increasingly isolated, increasingly enigmatic.

Maybe he was shocked by how readily the public consumed his music and wanted to give his fans something harder to digest, something they would have to work to attain. His appetite for reinvention made him prone to overdoing things. Critics accused him of being too white, too black, too sexual, too religious, too pop, too hard to understand, too mainstream, too out-there. Perhaps his singular talent overwhelmed him sometimes. Although he was able to play every instrument on his tracks, sing all the vocals and mix them together in his three personal studios, his best work was made in collaboration, not isolation. But it was isolation that he craved, as if only then could he see himself clearly.

He died alone in an elevator from an overdose of prescription pain pills, taken maybe for the muscles he tore performing breathtaking splits, or the bones he broke jumping off pianos and stages, or maybe something else; he was private. His own security cameras recorded his death, a man with a cane, in high heels, falling down with no one to catch him, a man who once sang:

Are we gonna let the elevator bring us down
Oh, no, let's go, go crazy
I said let's go, go crazy
Let's go, let's go, go, let's go

Dr. Everything'll Be Alright
Make everything go wrong
Pills and thrills and daffodils will kill
Hang tough children

He's comin'
He's comin'
Comin'

Take me away

The night before the surgery I wash my body with anti-bacterial Dial soap. In the morning, I wash again with the same orange bar. I pop a prescribed Valium to calm my nerves and pack a biography of Prince, *Dig If You Will the Picture*, because maybe I will wake lucid enough to read, and I want Prince to be the first thing through my post-op brain. I dress in the loose sweatpants and zip-up sweatshirt I bought for the occasion; they will be easy to take off when the post-op pain will prevent me from lifting my hands over my head. I do my hair in a series of tight braids because I know it will be days before I can reach up and comb it again.

It is early morning. Valium works fast, and despite being nervous, I surprise Daniel by turning up Prince on the CD player, and I'm still humming his lyrics as we check into the surgical center and I change into a hospital robe and compression tights. I ask Daniel to leave before I am taken into the pre-op exam room; I want to be alone, with my body, while the doctor opens up my gown and draws dotted lines down my breastbone and around my nipples, and as the nurse slips a needle into my vein. I get crazy tired and drift backward into purple, then black.

My greatest concern about the surgery was that my breasts wouldn't feel like my body. I live largely in my flesh, sweating, moving, lifting for a living as a farmer and fitness instructor, and I worried that the revision would constantly nag at me. Would I bend and feel their weight and know that they were an addition to my form? Would I bump into them with my arms, or knock them while sliding through a doorframe? Would I touch them and think *plastic,* feel them and think *salt water*? During my consultation with the surgeon, I read a list of concerns from a scribbled note I'd folded in my purse.

How long is recovery? *Six weeks.*

Will I be able to breastfeed? *Yes, most likely.*

How long will the implants last? *Fifteen years at least, maybe longer.*

What is the main complaint post-op? *Many patients wish they'd gotten larger implants.*

I hesitated to ask if they would feel like *me.* It seemed like such a metaphysical concern after our discussion of pain meds, scar tissues, CCs of saline, days off from work, and recovery bras.

Will they feel like my body? *The first weeks they'll be swollen and might feel foreign. You may look in the mirror and be surprised by your shape. Most women have sensation in the skin and nipples after the second day post-op. After six weeks you'll return to all your normal activities. Your brain will get used to seeing your new body. I've talked to patients a few*

*years after augmentation, and they say they forgot they had
surgery. I have to press them to recall that they have implants.*

Saline has the same concentration of salt to water as do blood
and tears, so it isn't too foreign to the body. If I were to punc-
ture or deflate an implant, the solution would run out harm-
lessly into my chest cavity. Somehow I took comfort in the
idea of sameness. The surgery would be a revision in kind, not
an uncanny shift.

There's a line in the Prince song "Peach" that stuck with me
like a mantra: "She was pure, every ounce, I was sure, when
her titties bounced." Maybe it was the perfect rhyme between
ounce (I was thinking very much of my body in terms of measurements) and *bounce.* Maybe it was friction of faith (purity)
with sexuality, binding the spiritual to the carnal. Maybe it
was the silly word *titties,* which seems so childish and makes
me smile every time. Or maybe it was that prior to surgery, I
didn't have a bouncy chest, and that post-surgery my breasts
would finally bounce. I loved the song, despite the silliness of
the word *titties,* despite the offense that others might take.

What was it about purity and breasts? Was it a sense of
freedom? I imagined a girl jumping happily, jumping rope,
jumping on a trampoline, her body rising and falling in space.
It's a sexual image if you look only at her breasts, but it's also
just an image of a form in motion, the honest physics of flesh
moving in space. There is purity to this up and down, both
the heaviness of the body and its strength to rise against the
force of gravity, if only for a moment. The grace of the thing,
its mortality and its higher reaching.

Prince judges the purity of a woman by her body's movement. I was taught early that a body wasn't to be judged, like

a book's cover, but I've grown increasingly skeptical of that idea. There is value in beauty, surely not singular worth, but a body is a composite of a life—its habits (good and bad), its history (scars and stories), its priorities (how do you wish to be seen?)—and working with bodies in the role of farmer and fitness instructor, I have come, like Prince, to read them closely and with respect. They can be curated.

Although I own several editions of *Leaves of Grass*, it is Galway Kinnell's slim volume, *The Essential Whitman*, that I love most. The book has been worn to pieces by my love. It has been chewed by puppies and stained by red wine and black tea. Its pages are dog-eared, marked with Post-it notes and underlines. It is only slightly taller than it is wide, a proportion that suits Whitman's extravagantly long lines. I purchased it a decade ago, mostly out of respect for Kinnell, a poet whose mysticism electrified my homescape in Vermont. What he did in this volume is surely some form of theft, some type of alchemy, turning one form into another out of pure hope. He loved Whitman, but, like a true lover, saw his great faults—his bad revisions, his ego, his celebrity—and how time can ruin original energy, turning electric poems into sputtering candles.

Whitman, he believed, was at fault for these revisions, turning back to rework poems written half a lifetime ago, an old man revisiting a young man's poetry. In those years Whitman's poetry was reviewed and rejoiced, celebrated and mocked. Adaptable as a cat, Whitman went back into the works and recreated them to the critics' liking, he made them sound poemier, he overworked his language, and he eliminated some of his brilliant oddities and replaced them with clichés. But Kinnell undid these revisions, taking what he liked from each of their forms, creating his own hybrid poems from all of Whitman's re-envisionings, so what the reader finds in *The*

Essential Whitman is Whitman strained through the mind of Kinnell with the intent to present the very best version Whitman's work.

This straining is an act of love, an act of respect, like polishing a statue back to copper brilliance. I read it more often than the original, for having been revised so carefully, its value has increased. Many hands have been upon it, shaping it, mending it, improving it, as a farmer is said to improve land by husbandry and toil.

Prince christened one of his first protégées Vanity. She was tall, dark, and curvy and wore lingerie on stage, her hair in a huge halo of curls. Hurt by Prince's other love affairs, she began drinking and using drugs, habits that repulsed Prince and drove him away. Later, he would give women names like Carmen Electra, Apollonia, Diamond, and Pearl. Unlike them, he was born with his exotic title, although it was given to him too. Prince Roger was his father's stage name during his days as a jazz musician, and he gave his first son this faux name, like a hand-me-down dream.

In 1993 Prince announced that he was changing his name to a glyph, a chimera of the male and female symbols. "It is an unpronounceable symbol whose meaning has not been identified. It's all about thinking in new ways, tuning in 2 a new free-quency," he wrote, but the change was also likely a rebellion against Warner Bros., who held the trademark to the name Prince and the masters of all the music he'd recorded under his contract with that label. The symbol allowed him to produce records under his new, unpronounceable name. The press quickly began referring to him as The Artist Formerly Known as Prince because the symbol was too burdensome for print. His press agents suggested that the keys O(+> could be clumsily assembled to approximate the artist's new name, or, upon request, that a free Prince font could be installed via floppy disk. Prince played a custom guitar in the shape of the symbol. He wrote the word *slave* on his cheek during performances to protest his recording contract. He sang into a microphone shaped like a pistol, holding the barrel to his mouth like a man on the brink of suicide.

In 2000, when the contract expired, Prince returned to the name Prince, although he kept the guitar and the symbol as part of his image. Male + Female: the perfect combination of sex, ambiguity, and struggle, both artful and highly produced. It was a required revision but, within his story, an important one. The symbol freed him, briefly, to be more than Prince.

The first thing I felt was the weight. The implants added a total of two pounds to my chest, and upon waking from the surgery, I sensed them sitting on my ribs. I was able to walk out an hour later and slide into the CR-V that Daniel had left idling for warmth outside the surgical center. I don't remember much from the ride, but I recall describing how cool the IV fluid felt when it first raced up my vein and how quickly I'd fallen out of consciousness. At home Daniel helped me crawl into bed, where I slept off the surgical medications until nightfall. The daylight outside my window faded. My throat was raw from the tubing that had been slipped down it. I called to Daniel, and he turned on the light and encouraged me to rise.

All the strength in my arms was gone, cut through the chest, so I sat up using only my lower abs and then pulled my legs over the side of the bed. We drove to pick up takeout, and I watched my chest pressing out further in my sweatshirt, the seatbelt swelling. I was tremendously thirsty. Pain snuck up slowly, and I took my medications before it became anything more than pressure. The book I'd packed sat heavily in my bag, unopened. I slept in a deeper place than I can ever remember going, just at the rim of a great hole my consciousness had entered under anesthesia, one step from the brink of death.

In the morning, Daniel kissed me before leaving for work, and then the house was empty, and I was alone with my body and its tending. I swung out of bed and let the blood in my head settle before walking across the hall to the bathroom. The doctor had warned me not to worry when I removed the bandages; I would be swollen and shiny and pink and not at all the finished product, but I had to look, I had to see the shape of myself. I unzipped my sweatshirt and gingerly peeled off the sleeves. My chest was bound with a tan ACE bandage, hooked together with teethed stays. I removed them, and they clattered to the floor. Then, carefully, I revealed myself to my reflection, one pass at a time, until I was exposed fully, my skin raw in the cool air.

Despite my breasts riding high on my chest, despite the shine of my skin like an overfilled balloon, despite the bloody stains on the bandages, despite the press of the implants on my muscles like a hundred heavy bench-press reps, despite how tight I felt, bound up inside with stitches and loops, my eyes saw that shape and told my brain that it was mine, and instantly I was inhabiting a body whose form was, just two days ago, a fantasy. Still damp from the shower, looking at my form in the mirror, I began to weep.

ACKNOWLEDGMENTS

Thank you to the publications where some of these essays first appeared, some in different forms: "A Deliberate Thing I Said Once to My Skin" (*Threepenny Review*), "On Plucking White Hairs" (*Sweet Lit*), "Hunger" (*Florida Review*), "Heartbeat" (*March Badness*), "On Running" (*Creative Nonfiction Magazine's True Story Edition*), "Election Day" (*Stoneslide Media*), "Live Find" (*Magazine Solstice*), "On Teaching Brian Doyle's 'Leap' to Students Born after 9/11" (*Assay*), "A Model Home" (*Essay Daily*), "Ink" (*Punctuate Magazine*), "Muse" (*New South*), "Green Thumb" (*Colorado Review*), "Polish" (*Hotel Amerika*), and "On Revision" (*Hotel Amerika*).

Of the sources I've used here, I want to recognize those whose words give voice to these essays. Lines by Walt Whitman, Galway Kinnell, Gary Snyder, Hunter S. Thompson, Meriwether Lewis and William Clark, Brian Doyle, J. R. R. Tolkien, Bruce Springsteen, Patti Smith, Pablo Neruda, and Prince all appear in this book and often served to spark an idea. Their words, books, and songs are beloved, and some appear inked on my skin.

This book was made possible by the insight, wit, and support of writers, teachers, and friends. I want to thank Vermont College of the Fine Arts, where these essays first spilled onto the page, and Patrick Madden specifically, who encouraged their expansive weirdness and offered keen observations and suggestions that turned a jumble of research, obsessions, and literature into the collection contained in this book. Thank you too to all the editors who believed in these pieces and helped me polish and refine their roving hunger. Thank you to my wonderful workshop at Breadloaf's Environmental Writing Conference, where some of these pieces were completed. Thank you to family and friends, to dogs, to farms, and to authors I hold dear.

Above all, thank you to Daniel, whose love, support, and conversation are so present in these essays.

21ST CENTURY ESSAYS
David Lazar and Patrick Madden, Series Editors

This series from Mad Creek Books is a vehicle to discover, publish, and promote some of the most daring, ingenious, and artistic nonfiction. This is the first and only major series that announces its focus on the essay—a genre whose plasticity, timelessness, popularity, and centrality to nonfiction writing make it especially important in the field of nonfiction literature. In addition to publishing the most interesting and innovative books of essays by American writers, the series publishes extraordinary international essayists and reprint works by neglected or forgotten essayists, voices that deserve to be heard, revived, and reprised. The series is a major addition to the possibilities of contemporary literary nonfiction, focusing on that central, frequently chimerical, and invariably supple form: The Essay.

*Annual Gournay Prize Winner